Ann Helen Unger
Walter Unger

Pagodas, Gods and Spirits of Vietnam

Thames and Hudson

Contents

Pictures on previous pages:

Page 1: Ornamental garden and seven-storey stupa at the
Thien Mu pagoda in Hue

Pages 2 and 3: The Ngoc Son *den*, a memorial temple on
Hoan Kiem Lake, Hanoi

Pages 4 and 5: Pilgrims' boats on their way to the Huong
pagoda, south of Hanoi

Page 6: Statue of Quan Am, the Goddess of Mercy, in the
garden of the Pho Minh pagoda, Rach Gia, Mekong Delta

Page 7: Decoration at the entrance to the Tran Hung Dao
hero temple, Saigon

Pages 8 and 9: Gateway to the Bich Dong mountain pagoda
near Ninh Hai, North Vietnam

Page 10: Buddha sculpture in the Jade Emperor pagoda,
Saigon

Pagodas, Gods and Spirits of Vietnam

Old traditions revived

They start arriving in the early morning, before the sun is covered by clouds of mist and another grey day begins in the north of Vietnam. Then more and more appear, travelling east from Hanoi along Highway 18 in a procession of ramshackle vehicles, turning off at the small town of Uong Bi on to a gravel track broken by rocky river courses leading north into the mountains.

Most of them look worn out, men and women with callused hands and backs bent from a lifetime working in the rice fields. But their faces are radiant and even having to push their vehicles across deep fords does not dampen their spirits. They are realizing the dream of a lifetime – the pilgrimage to Yen Tu Mountain. It has been a shrine for the Vietnamese since kings of the Tran dynasty retired into seclusion there in their old age seven centuries ago, to become monks and study the Buddha's teachings. One of the kings, Tran Nhan Tong, is buried there.

It was not only their devoutness that made these rulers venerable figures of worship for the Vietnamese. Like so many others who became heroes and heroines in the defensive and liberation wars that have permeated the country's history, the Tran kings were immortalized by their earthly deeds as well. Their victorious battles against the invading hordes of the Mongol Kublai Khan gave them, Prince Tran Hung Dao in particular, a godlike status and respect that remain undiminished even now.

After jolting along the road for 15 kilometres the pilgrims reach their destination, a huge, dusty square lined with stalls halfway up the 1,000-metre

Pilgrims' path on Yen Tu Mountain

high mountain. If they have not brought offerings and walking equipment with them they can buy them here: incense sticks and medicinal roots, rice cakes and fruit, garlands of flowers and bamboo staffs to help them keep their footing on the hard road ahead.

A picturesque landscape opens out. The thick dark green of the banana bushes alternates with the soft greenery of bamboo groves and the gnarled trunks of the ancient pine forest. With every step up the mountain the view across boundless hills widens. A steep path with an uneven rocky surface leads to the first place of pilgrimage, the Suoi Tam, the Stream of the Purifying Bath. Here, according to tradition, the Tran kings washed away the

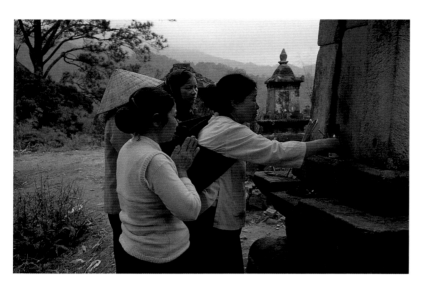

Women lighting incense in the stupa garden

impurities of the physical world before beginning their lives as monks. Immediately behind, surrounded by weathered stupas, is the fasting pagoda of Cam Thuc, in which Tran Nhan Tong ate his first vegetarian meal.

Crossing narrow passes, deep ravines, watercourses and eroded tree roots, the path winds on up to temples, shrines and stupa gardens. Monks and nuns meet the arrivals in front of the altars, which are shrouded in incense and covered with offerings. Breathlessly the pilgrims listen to the stories familiar to them all since childhood: the Pagoda of the Innocent Souls, built on the spot where the court ladies who travelled with Tran Nhan Tong jumped to their death because they could not bear to leave him; the peaceful death of the ruler who lay down to die in a misty glade, where the Cloud Temple was later built; the Tuong Yen Ky Sinh, a rock in the shape of a woman's body, which still bears the name of the peasant woman An Ky Sinh, martyred in the war of liberation against the Chinese invaders.

At each of the sacred places the visitors light their incense sticks, leave their offerings and pray, give the nuns and monks a modest donation from their savings and then stand still with heads bowed in reverence. In Vietnamese popular religion, hero kings or freedom fighters, Taoist saints or Buddhas and their helpers, all on the same altar, all have the same power to protect and help, they are all due the same respect. It is not only Yen Tu Mountain that attracts a never-ending stream of believers; people also flock to the countless other places of pilgrimage all over the country.

Every spring hundreds of thousands of people gather on Nghia Linh mountain north-west of Hanoi to pray to the godlike Au Co, the primal mother whose eldest son founded the legendary Hung dynasty many years ago. Another place of pilgrimage in the north of the country, in the middle of a river landscape full of curiously shaped limestone hills, is Chua Huong, the Perfume Pagoda, a collection of temple buildings and stalactite caves where believers pray for salvation and blessing to Buddhist and Taoist sacred figures alike. Just as many people visit the shrines in the centre and south of the country, such as the Hon Chen Temple of the Mother Goddess in Hue and Black Lady Mountain near Saigon, where ancient sacred stones, Hindu religious relics from the old Cham empire and the Goddess of Mercy Qhan Am, who has Buddhist roots, exist harmoniously side by side.

It is clear from the crowds flocking to the sacred sites that religious belief is still deep-rooted in the Vietnamese, although the Communist government tried for several decades to suppress it. In fact since the late 1980s, when the country was opened up and people were once again allowed to practise their religion, there has been an upsurge of interest in history and traditional beliefs which is by no means confined to the older generation.

Most Vietnamese, when asked what religion they are, say Buddhist. In books, too, Vietnam is often described as a Buddhist country. But in fact the popular religion which is now being practised so actively again is an inextricable mixture of religious beliefs and philosophies. Early this century the French writer Leopold Michel Cadière described it as an impenetrable forest: 'You see gigantic tree trunks sinking their roots into unknown depths; the impenetrable canopy of leaves forms dark shadowy vaults; the branches bend to the ground and put out new roots; climbing plants twine from tree to tree – you can see no beginning and no end . . .' The same would be true even today.

The source and core of this popular belief have always been the ancestor cult and the animistic worship of spirits which governed the life, death and day-to-day existence of men for a good 2,000 years before recorded history began. It was only later that the other three components which still remain a major influence on religious belief arrived in the country: Taoism, the nature doctrine of the Chinese philosopher Lao-tse; Confucianism, the rules of the Chinese political and moral teacher Kung-fu-tse; and Buddhism, the enlightenment doctrine of Siddhartha Gautama, originating in India and brought to Vietnam and China by monks.

Taoism and Confucianism came with the Chinese occupying forces who subjugated the north of Vietnam around the turn of the Christian era. Buddhism arrived in the same way, but also by another route; with Buddhist Indian sailors and the monks travelling with them, who stopped on the Vietnamese coast on their trading voyages across the China Sea. The people and their rulers, demoted by the Chinese to colonial princes, never ceased trying to free themselves from the political oppression and economic exploitation, but they accepted the imported religions without resistance.

This was less illogical than it might appear. At the beginning the new teachings did not directly affect the peasants, who could not read and write. They believed that their fate was entirely in the hands of the good or evil spirits, which they continued to worship. The inevitable religious and political debates were between the rulers and their educated administrators, together with the

Chinese monks, who increasingly were settling on the Red River in the colony. Moreover, a characteristically Vietnamese trait was already emerging – a readiness to adopt from foreign influences anything that might be useful and improve their own lot.

From the beginning the Vietnamese have had to struggle harder for their existence than any other nation in South-East Asia. Not only did they have to fight for their independence for two thousand years; their existence has been a constant battle for survival against powerful and threatening forces of nature. As a result they welcomed any divine help, which Buddhism and Taoism promised in particular. As rice growers they lived in constant anxiety about their harvests, under threat of storms, drought and floods – which explains not only why they pray to the spirits inherent in all these forces of nature but also their ambivalent relationship with their neighbour, China: on the one hand they still fear Chinese intervention but during the 1,000-year occupation they came to respect Chinese achievements such as the damming of rivers and the irrigation of fields.

Ancestor worship: memorial tablets on the family altar

Like the constant alternation of day and night, rain and drought in nature, like the never-ending cycle of work and rest, sowing and harvesting in earthly existence, in Vietnamese religion human life is a process of constant renewal, which does not stop with death. *Hon* and *via*, higher- and lower-ranking souls, take over a person's body when he is born and leave him when he dies. So death simply means moving to another existence. 'Passed away', the expression so often used in the West to announce the loss of a relative, is incomprehensible to a Vietnamese; when his father or grandmother dies he has not lost them. The duty of younger members of the family to show respect

A traditional wedding. The bride's father is kneeling in front of the family altar.

to their elders does not end with the older person's death and vice versa; the dead are not released from their family responsibilities when they die.

This idea is expressed in the strongest and deepest root of Vietnamese religious belief: ancestor worship. No ritual is more important. The most honoured place in the house is reserved for the ancestors' altar. The souls of the dead, embodied in memorial tablets on the altar, continue to play a part in family life. They are always served at festive meals; the altar is never without flowers and incense. They are asked for advice and protection for every family event – marriage or birth, school exam or business deal.

Vietnamese society is changing, becoming more and more industrialized and motorized, and many young people are moving to the towns. But most of the population still lives in the countryside, usually with the whole family under one roof. These days the dead are usually buried in public cemeteries and not in graves in their own rice field as they used to be; increasingly they are cremated and buried in urns rather than coffins. It is no longer a matter of course for the son to learn the ceremonial rites of death and burial and pass them on later to his own son; nowadays professional masters of ceremonies are often used. But in both the towns and the countryside, ancestor worship is a binding duty for every Vietnamese, the ancestor altar is the centre of the family, the symbol of its cohesion.

The two most important wishes in the lives of the Vietnamese are that they should have at least one son and die in his presence. Patients about to die in hospital ask to be taken home if possible to die in the bosom of their family. Their souls cannot find peace unless their relations accompany them on their final journey. The most important requirement when a person dies is a piece of white silk, the *hon bach*, the Cloth of the White Soul. It is laid on the dying person's chest and immediately he breathes his last is tied around the soul to capture it, in a shape resembling a human figure with head and limbs. This is followed by the *phan nam*, the 'rice in mouth' ritual, symbolic food for the journey to the other world.

The cement-sealed coffins often used to be kept in the house for a week, to allow geomancers, experts versed in the earth and the cosmos, to determine the right day for burial from the position of the stars and the most favourable burial place from the topographical conditions. These days, old people have often chosen their burial place in advance, but they still consult geomancers, who tell them where they will be best hidden from evil spirits. So even today graves are not arranged in straight lines in Vietnam; most burial mounds, surrounded by oval walls, are scattered around the cemetery in no apparent order.

The custom of burial as an important ceremonial family occasion has survived, in many villages with the help of burial associations. Not only do these provide the magnificent hearses, now usually motorized, painted with coloured dragons, clouds and flowers, their members also act as ceremonial helpers, pall-bearers and musicians; they swing incense and wave flags. Wearing white cloths around their heads as a sign of mourning, they assemble at the dead person's house as the coffin is lifted on to the hearse and monks pray. Bamboo poles are clashed together, muffled drumrolls sounded, to keep evil spirits away; red banners are unfurled with the titles and merits of the deceased on them in white or gold letters. Everyone has his place in the procession, which then proceeds slowly to the burial place. At the front are the monks, protected by yellow lacquered parasols. They are followed by helpers dressed in black or blue robes. They carry the soul cloth on a small table with the wooden memorial tablet about 30 centimetres high, already inscribed by the village artist with the person's name and dates of birth and death. After them come the musicians and then the family – the eldest son in front of the coffin, the other members of the family behind.

At the edge of the cemetery the coffin is lifted from the hearse and carried to the grave on the helpers' shoulders. Then comes the most important ritual: as the coffin is lowered into the grave the scribe makes a red dot with a paintbrush on the memorial tablet – this completes the symbolic unification of the dead person's soul with the family and integration into the long chain of ancestors and future generations.

But the duty to remember and honour the dead does not end with burial. The dates of subsequent ceremonies are precisely laid down. On the third day after the funeral the children return to the grave to burn incense and banknotes and bring a meal from the family kitchen. The fifth day is the beginning of *man khoc*, an end to tears. On the 50th and the 100th day the family members all gather again for memorial rites at the family altar. After that the ancestors are paid the same respects as all the generations of the dead on the tablets at the shrine – on the dead person's birthday, on all religious feast days and on *tet*, New Year's Day, a particularly elaborate ceremony.

But what happens to the souls of those who do not die peacefully in the bosoms of their families, die a sudden or violent death or have no family?

Hearse decorated with dragons and flowers

They face the most terrible fate that can befall a soul in Vietnamese popular religion, roaming restlessly as *ma* or *qui*, evil spirits. In the spirit world, which is closely linked to ancestor worship, they are seen as especially dangerous. They can appear maliciously anywhere without warning, always ready to waylay people, kill them and steal their souls so that they can share in the homage they have forfeited.

There are field and wayside shrines all over the country dedicated to these lost souls. To appease them passers-by light incense or leave offerings, more through fear than sympathy. These shrines are particularly frequent on Highway 1, especially along the hazardous mountain pass between Da Nang and Hue, where drivers throw a few coins out of the window to buy the protection of the spirits.

In the last war, with its millions of frequently anonymous deaths and the waves of refugees which tore many families apart, many Vietnamese could no longer perform their duties to their ancestors and the responsibility was often taken over by monks. In a number of pagodas there are altars covered with photos of the dead and the monks are paid to say the prescribed prayers on the anniversary of their death. Another problem for the urban Vietnamese, creating a moral conflict between

Urn shrine in the Khan Van Nam Vien pagoda, Saigon

duty to the ancestors and practicality, is that as the towns grow larger there is less room in the cemeteries for burial places. To their way of thinking, having to cremate the dead is sacrilege. As a result some pagodas in large cities, such as the Khan Van Nam Vien in Saigon, have taken on a new role; in special rooms built for the purpose, urns containing the ashes of the dead are stored on hundreds of shelves and again it is left to the monks to pay them the necessary respects if the families are no longer able to.

Animism: life in two worlds

A farmer in the village of An Cuu, wanting to repair his house, cut a dozen bamboo poles and put them in a pool for a couple of weeks to remove vermin. The wood soon began to give off a musty smell. When neighbours complained, the farmer leaned the poles against the trunk of a nearby banyan tree to dry. The next night he had a terrible pain and suddenly, while he was half asleep, he heard a voice. 'This is my resting place,' it whispered. 'You have disturbed me with your bamboo and I am going to punish you.'

The man, terrified, realized that he must have offended a spirit. That same night he went and stood outside the door and bowed down towards the tree with his hands clasped in front of his chest to beg forgiveness. In the morning he had the poles removed; he then sent for an old woman experienced in dealing with genies to ask for her help in finding out which spirit he had offended. The sorceress lit incense and set out various herbs and then lay down under the leafy canopy of the banyan tree. After praying for a long time, first in a murmur and then in more and more imploring tones, she jumped up and cried, 'I am Ba Hoa. This tree belongs to me. I will forgive you this time, but I want you to bring me sacrifices!'

Then the farmer realized he had been in great danger, because this spirit, of all those that continually threaten the Vietnamese, was the one least to be trifled with. Ba Hoa is the female fire spirit, particularly feared by people living in wooden buildings and always addressed as *ba* (lady). The farmer, barely recovered, carried out his promise. He built a straw-covered hut by the tree trunk and set up a small altar there.

This myth from the village of An Cuu in the central Vietnamese province of Thua Thien Hue is just one of many showing how closely the everyday life of the whole people is bound up with a host of spirits. In the villages and towns, in the mountains and on the rice field plains, the children grow up from an early age with these ever-changing stories, which make the abstract and incomprehensible comprehensible. The belief in spirits is not confined to old people or simple peasants; young people and educated, cultured city dwellers live, though to differing degrees, in the same dualistic world as their ancient ancestors – the natural, real world and the supernatural world of forces which can be felt but not seen. Like the living souls in ancestor worship, the omnipresent genies govern the lives of the Vietnamese day and night.

Spirits, female and male, good and evil, are everywhere. They hover through the air and ride on the winds. They swim in the seas and glide

Tiger relief on a protective pagoda wall, around 1900

through the rivers, they are enthroned on mountain peaks and hide in the depths of ravines. They live on trees and under stones, appear in various forms, often as animals such as dragons, tigers or whales; they rule over all parts of heaven and earth. The tiger in particular, feared as much as he is admired, is greatly revered. Protective walls decorated with tiger reliefs are often built outside pagodas and temples.

To win the indulgence of the spirits or secure their good will is as indispensable for the Vietnamese as their daily bread. In the centre and south of the country it is an old custom to set up small shrines outside the houses where respect is paid to the genies with incense sticks and gifts of food. In the north, garden gates and house doors are often decorated with mirrors to ward off harmful forces. On trees in the towns, boundary stones in the villages, rocks on remote mountain

paths or footpaths in the rice fields, the Vietnamese pay tribute to the spirits in a thousand ways, by lighting incense or leaving a couple of flowers. Every fishing boat has its decorated altar and no lorry driver would set out without the protection of a healing amulet. When families go on a journey, they call on a protective patron. Particularly popular are the legendary General Quan Cong, who is found in many pagodas, and the Chinese military leader Tran Vu in the temple named after him in Hanoi. The devout stroke their statues while praying, then stroke themselves and their children on the head and body to transfer the blessing of the guardian spirit.

In the provinces in northern and central Vietnam there are a number of shrines, small temples or open brick altars dedicated to a *tho than*, an earth spirit, who reveals himself by letting a single tree grow up in the open countryside. No farmer would think of cutting the tree down or tilling the field. He and the whole village community see the tree as a sign that the spirit is waiting for offerings at this spot. Every 1st and 15th day of the lunar month, the farmers place a dish of rice, a cup of tea or rice wine on this *am* and, in more elaborate ceremonies before the field is ploughed and before the rice harvest, more lavish gifts such

Freshly decorated shrine for a stone spirit

Field shrine between rice fields near Hue

as garlands of flowers, gold- or silver-coloured banknotes.

Dealing with the genies is complicated by the fact that they have a hierarchy. Apart from the countless local spirits, often ruling just a single tree or stone, the next in the hierarchy are the male spirits who protect the village, venerated by the men in community houses. The village women have their own sacred figures, often females from history or legend, distinguished by their particularly virtuous lives or as miracle healers. They are prayed to in their own shrines in the pagoda

Sorceresses and sorcerers to conjure up spirits, around 1920

grounds, recognizable by the coloured women's hats with which they are decorated.

At the top of the hierarchy are the spirits ruling over the major spheres of influence, matter and the elements: rain, drought, mountains, rivers, earth. The highest is Ong Troi, the ruler of heaven. Until the Vietnamese monarchy came to an end in 1945 only the king or the emperor was allowed to worship him and the other major rulers of the spirit world. Every year they held a spectacular offering ceremony at the Nam Giao, the altar of heaven and earth, on behalf of the whole nation.

Unfortunately evil spirits are very much in the majority in this Vietnamese spirit world. They may be low-ranking but there are huge numbers of them and they cause most of the daily problems in the lives of the Vietnamese. Not only are they sly, they are also hypersensitive, vengeful and capricious. Tirelessly they lie in wait, taking advantage of any opportunity to do harm. However honest a person might be, however hard working and thrifty, he is always at risk of crossing an evil spirit. Often he does not realize until it is too late. When the axe goes into the woodcutter's leg, has he taken away a wood spirit's resting place? When the farmer's rice is killed by drought, has he not shown the water spirits proper respect? When the tradesman's business fails, has he incurred the displeasure of his trade's guardian spirit? Is the woman who loses her child the victim of a *ba co*, the restless roaming spirit of an aunt who died unmarried?

Often the people affected cannot even see which action or failing incurred the displeasure of which spirit. But fortunately help is at hand in such cases from the *ba dong* and *ong dong*, sorcerers and sorceresses who have usually passed on their knowledge from generation to generation in their own families. How they discover which evil spirit was responsible for a stroke of misfortune remains their secret. In occult rituals which demonstrate the ability of the Vietnamese to believe in the mythical and expedient at the same time, they put right the troubled relationship between the human being and the supernatural adversary.

Magicians are still consulted in many villages and even in the capital, Hanoi, although their importance is diminishing. Hardly anyone in Vietnam now believes in sacrifice, which used to be recommended as a gesture of reconciliation with the spirits. If possible the sacrificial animal must be killed on a river bank so that its blood – a substitute for the blood of the person the spirit had a grudge against – could flow away with the water and lure the demon on to a false track. The belief that evil forces are particularly inclined to single out firstborn children has also died out. At one time it was customary to refer to the first child as number two at all the ceremonies for his protection, to confuse the evil spirits. For the same reason boys, still seen in Asian cultures as 'more precious', were dressed in girls' clothes until they had passed the most dangerous age. Often children were provisionally given ugly-sounding names so that they were not picked on – which caused great confusion when the French colonial bureaucrats introduced accurate registers of births.

It was mainly their knowledge of medicinal herbs and roots that gave the spirit experts a reputation for miracle-working in the old days. This has since been overtaken by modern medicine, but even now the Vietnamese do not put their trust in it completely. For instance the spirits are still feared at births, even when they take place in hospital. Many families still follow the tradition that a young mother returns to her parents' house to spend a hundred days in seclusion in a closed room. According to the ancient belief this is the only way she can be safe from harmful winds. Behind the belief lies a fear of influences which were thought to be evil spirits of the air – before they were scientifically proved to be dangerous bacteria and viruses.

Many of the rules that have traditionally been associated with house building also survive. Obvi-

Owner of a new house praying at an offertory table

ously the Vietnamese now rely on architects and engineers when they are having a house built. But they also seek the advice of the old-fashioned geomancer, although he does sometimes use a helicopter nowadays to survey the land. And he certainly never forgets – just to be on the safe side – the prescribed invocations of the spirits when the building work begins.

The first stage is a solemn ritual on the site. In front of a table altar laden with sacrifices, the builder prostrates himself on the ground several times and asks his ancestors to sanction the building of the house. The craftsmen then seek the blessing of their protective patron. Before the first stone is laid, before the supporting pillars are erected, after the roof is completed and before the bricks are laid – very similar to Western practices such as the laying of the foundation stone and topping-out – further ceremonies follow, dedicated to the various earth, air, garden, wood or stone-spirits and similar in form: 'Today is a lucky day and we beg the . . . spirit to accept our humble gifts and give us approval for the building of this house.' The usual gifts such as incense sticks, rice, flowers and fruit are offered on the altar.

The most important act for the future of the house used to be *le tong moc*, banishing demons from the rafters. People used to make little paper houses with banknotes stuck on to them and five little straw dolls inside representing the evil forces. The owner of the house took this to the river with his family and threw the little house into the water; if there was no river nearby it was burnt. This drove out the evil spirits. Although this ceremony has now died out, *le lac thanh*, celebrating the completion of the building, is still the custom. If the house owner is prosperous enough a cooked pig is donated, which the foremen of the carpenters and bricklayers share between them and take home. After that there is no further obstacle to the family's future happiness in the new house.

The most senior ancestor and spirit princes used to be given noble titles and qualifications carved on tablets and steles with which the rulers hoped to secure the protection of the supernatural forces for their people. This custom has died out since 1945, when the last emperor of the Nguyen dynasty abdicated. But Vietnamese of all classes still feel the need to subordinate themselves to the spirits, they still respect the supernatural with a mixture of veneration and fear. Many superstitions have survived into modern times – for instance the belief that no one should start an important project on the 5th, 14th and 23rd day of the month. No one knows where this originated, but even Vietnamese who have been living abroad for a long time still abide by it.

Taoism: distant paradises and holy mothers

When Taoism reached Vietnam with the Chinese occupying forces in the first two centuries before and after Christ, it had already evolved considerably from the original concept of Tao, the way to inner harmony between man and nature. In place of the clear, uncompromising philosophy of its earlier exponents, it was by then intermingled with spirit beliefs and magic cults – which made the Vietnamese people all the more receptive to it.

The idea of Tao had developed five hundred years earlier, at the time of the Warring States. China was divided into several feudal empires whose feuding led to serious political crises and social unrest. The search for solutions produced two strongly contrasting doctrines: Confucianism and Taoism. In one the well-being of the state and its people is subject to a rigid system of rule based on moral principles; the other advocates the self-realization of the individual.

Whereas Confucian ideas can be traced back to the historical figure Kung-fu-tse, the political and moral teacher, the origins of Taoism are lost in the mists of time. There is no doubt that it originated generally from the philosopher Lao-tse (Old Master) but very little is known about him. There is no monument providing any information. According to tradition he was a contemporary of Confucius and administrator of the archives in Lo-yang, the capital of the state of Chou. The assumption that Lao-tse wrote the *Tao Te Ching*, the book 'Of the way and its power', the basic Taoist work, is also based on legend. It is said that when the master, weary of the unrest in the world, wanted to retreat to the seclusion of the forests, he

Statue of the philosopher Lao-tse in the Khan Van Nam Vien *chua*, Saigon

was asked by royal guards to write down his thoughts.

The nucleus of these ideas is the recognition that if man truly wants to be free he must adapt himself to Tao. Tao is the incomprehensible natural force which all events in the universe, the macrocosm or the microcosm, unfailingly follow – the rising and setting of the sun and moon, the changing seasons, the blossoming and fading of the flowers. Tao is the harmony inherent in the whole of nature, which earlier Chinese thinkers had already expressed as *yin* and *yang* and depicted as two shapes intertwined in a closed circle, one dark, the other light, with each having the colour of the other at one point, showing the inseparability of the two parts. They symbolize the energies which generate and are dependent on each other: shade and light, cold and warmth, stillness and movement, water and fire, woman and man.

In Tao philosophy, any human intervention merely disrupts the natural harmony of all being. According to a verse in the *Tao Te Ching*, 'I have found that any attempt to conquer and manipulate the world is a failure. He who manipulates it destroys it. He who tries to capture it loses it.' Later Tao thinkers, particularly the contentious Chuang-tzu (369–286 BC), concentrated the somewhat fatalistic view of life into a strong plea to reject subservience. For them, feudal rule and the Confucian system of government, the compulsion to learn and civil obedience were artificial constructs and as such simply caused disputes, hypocrisy and misery. Their practical solution, applicable to the crises of their time, was a return to nature. Only in perfect harmony with Tao can man be at peace with himself and the universe.

The highly philosophical, abstract Tao debate of the intellectual elite had no relevance for the peasants. But exponents who brought Taoism to the people in new and understandable forms soon appeared in China and its colonies. They were not afraid to borrow many elements of Buddhism,

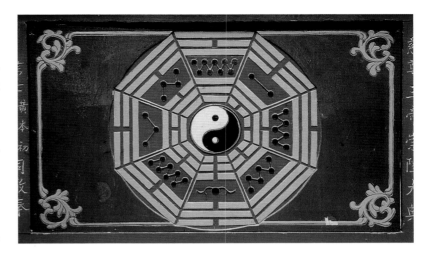

Diagrams and yin and yang symbols from the Chinese oracle book *I Ching*

which was establishing itself as an independent religion at the same time. They not only copied the sutras, the Buddhist scriptures, but also adopted the concepts of rebirth, the judges of hell and salvation.

To the numerous existing spirits these Taoist priests added an ever-growing number of other figures of worship personified as gods: the Jade Emperor who lives in heaven as the highest creator and controller of the universe, divine mothers worshipped as givers of fertility, earthly heroes with miraculous powers. Natural phenomena, animals and beings from the world of mythology were also deified and included in the pantheon: stars, each with their equivalent in earthly matter, for instance Mercury = water, Venus = metal, Jupiter = wood; tigers whose names men can scarcely utter from fear, but whose protective power can be invoked by magicians; dragons which, in Vietnamese mythology, rule the seas and carry whole stretches of land on their gigantic armour.

Promises of immortality preceded by a long life on earth in happiness, health and prosperity also bore no relation to the original idea of Tao. People listened fascinated to tales of distant paradises, islands of bliss in the eastern seas. Increasingly the priests presented themselves as soothsayers and mediums providing a link to guardian deities and threatening spirits for believers. As alchemists they mixed miracle elixirs, as healers they devised allegedly life-prolonging diets and breathing techniques, as magicians they supplied amulets and coloured strips of papers with secret signs whose contents the peasants did not understand, but they trusted in their power.

The deities that emerged at that time are still worshipped by the Vietnamese. But for many of them it is difficult to say, after several centuries of intermingling, whether they are of Taoist origin or came from the existing pantheon. This is true in particular of the deified heroes and heroines, many of whom were adopted by the Taoist priests and had new legends woven about them. The Vietnamese also simply adopted natural spirits which they already regarded as gods and included them in their own heavenly hierarchy.

The kitchen god Ong Tao, who even today plays an important part in popular belief, is a legacy of Taoism. The story of his origins is a tragedy which begins with a man who left his wife because he could not have children. Unhappily he roamed around the world. After many years he chanced to return to his old village, but without recognizing his house or his wife. She, however, having in the meantime remarried, recognized him and gave him a bowl of rice out of sympathy. At that moment the new husband appeared. The wife, fearing that he would misunderstand the situation, hid the homecomer in a heap of old straw. Then disaster struck: the husband, not realizing he was there, put the straw on the fire. The wife, stricken with guilt, threw herself on the fire. Her husband tried to save her but all three perished in the flames.

The three tragic figures are symbolized by the three stones or lumps of clay which are still used to put the pots on in country fireplaces. But even many modern kitchens have a shrine to the kitchen god as well as a gas or electric cooker. He is worshipped there every day, but once a year he is the centre of attention. On the 23rd day of the last lunar month he goes up to heaven to report to the Jade Emperor on his family. Parents and children gather in the kitchen to say goodbye to Ong Tao. They adorn him with a white paper cap, coloured garments and flowers. They also used to release a carp they had caught previously and the kitchen god set off on his journey on its back – all expressions of respect intended to persuade him to put in a good word for the family with the Jade Emperor.

Vietnam has no exclusively Taoist pagodas, although there are some in which Taoism is the dominant element. The most famous is the Ngoc Hoang in Saigon. Permanently wreathed in dense clouds of incense and guarded by stern figures of warriors, the Jade Emperor presides over a collection of colourfully decorated demigods and helpers. He is flanked by the star gods Nam Tao and Bac Dau, who according to popular belief keep the register of births and deaths. The white-robed figure of Than Tai, the bringer of good fortune, reputed to pay back donations of money many times over, is especially popular. Twelve Holy Women dressed in red and always surrounded by burning offertory candles also have many visitors. Holding children carefully in their arms, they stand for goodness and love, whereas drinking and neglecting their offspring they symbolize hardheartedness and selfishness – a warning to mothers.

In the same pagoda is a typical example of how the Taoists borrowed one element of the Buddhist religion and then embellished it in their own way – the underworld of the ten kings of hell. Depicted on two large panels, they supervise the enforcement of punishments for every possible type of earthly behaviour. The cruellest tortures, graphically illustrated by the wood carvers, are meted out to the sinners. Quacks or fraudulent priests are beheaded, torn apart, speared with iron bars; counterfeiters or bigamists are crushed with grind-

Quan Am, the Goddess of Mercy, saviour from the torments of hell

stones, immersed in vats of boiling oil, pierced with arrows; adulterous or cheating women have their stomachs slit open, their tongues cut out, their bodies thrown to hungry tigers and dogs.

The Goddess of Mercy Quan Am, also derived from Buddhism, appears in the horrific scenes as a saviour and can intervene in these tortures, since good deeds are also taken into account in the judgment. The kings of hell can shorten the way through the torture chambers for those who sinned but also helped the sick and the poor or gave money to monasteries and speed up the cycle of the transmigration of souls for them.

The worship of the Thanh Mau, the Holy Mothers, already very important from the spiritual beginnings of Vietnamese popular religion, was strongly influenced by Taoism. In nearly all pagodas they have their own places of prayer, visited mainly by women. The most senior of these goddesses are Lieu Hanh, ruler of the earth, her

sister Thoai, who watches over seas, rivers and springs, and Thuong Ngan, who rules over mountains and forests. They are obeyed not only by phalanxes of female servants but also by male assistants – clear evidence for religious experts that this hierarchy evolved long before the influence of foreign religions, when the early inhabitants of what later became Vietnam still had a matriarchal system. The fact that the Vietnamese have always traced their origins back to a woman, the legendary primal mother Au Co who is still revered today, is further evidence of that. On all visits to pagodas and pilgrimages, prayers in the *dien*, in front of the mother altar usually guarded by five tigers, are at least as important for Vietnamese women as prayers to the Buddha.

Recently *len dong*, appeals to the spirits by women for women, have become more common again. Laden with offerings they gather around a wise woman wrapped in white or red robes by her followers, who goes into a trance with prayers and invocations, often helped along by betel, tobacco and alcohol. The medium gets up, begins the seance by dancing and starts communing with the spirits in a strange voice. Often these secret meetings last for hours until all the questions that the participants have for particular spirits have been

Carved scene of hell in the Ngoc Hoang *chua*, Saigon

put and answered; then the medium sinks down exhausted and returns to this world.

At the very beginning of his reign in the early 19th century the emperor Gia Long made all these rituals punishable, regarding them as witchcraft and trickery which would corrupt the people. Mediums were threatened with 100 strokes and six months' forced labour. But one of his successors, Dong Khanh, revoked the ban ninety years later. He himself often took part in such ceremonies in the Hon Chen temple dedicated to the cult of the mother not far from the emperor's palace in Hue. When the Communists came to power in the north in 1945 and in the south in 1975 all religious activities, including the spirit meetings, came to an end. But now, anachronistic though it might seem, they are experiencing an unexpected revival.

Confucianism: cosmic order and moral standards

The peaceable doctrine of Confucianism, which still influences Vietnamese popular religion and political thought, started with an act of war: the occupation of the mountain and delta region on the Red River by troops of the Chinese Han dynasty in 111 BC. It was the beginning of an era characterized by cruelty and exploitation, which lasted 1,000 years and to this day gives the Vietnamese an ambivalent attitude to their giant neighbour, China. At the same time it was a turning point in the cultural history of the peasants, who had until then been illiterate. The occupiers brought technical progress and innovations in agriculture, dam building and artificial irrigation, water buffaloes and iron ploughshares. They also established a system of administration by mandarins which shaped Vietnam's government for the next 2,000 years. The strict training and loyalty demanded from these officials, dating back to the Chinese teacher Confucius, and

Statue of the moral teacher Confucius in the Temple of Literature, Hanoi

indeed the whole Confucian way of thought, concentrating on morality and the preservation of tradition, lasted longer in Vietnam than in China where it originated.

Kung-fu-tse (551–479 BC), whose name was latinized to Confucius by Jesuit missionaries in the 17th century, grew up in a village near Qufu in what is now the province of Shantung. All that is known of his father is that he died at the age of seventy, soon after his son's birth. His mother tried to give her son the best possible education. The village teachers taught him reading, writing, arithmetic and music. With great success: by the time he was twenty he had secured a position as a scribe for the State government.

At the time, China was going through a period of wars and social unrest. The Zhou dynasty, which four centuries earlier had united the empire in a federation under which it flourished, was losing its power. New feudal dynasties were fighting for supremacy and attacking neighbouring states. The political and social structure created during the Zhou period, based on allegiances, disintegrated. The moral code, creating a bond between the rulers and their dependents in reciprocal obligations, broke down. Alongside the Tao philosophy, in which the way to salvation lay in the renunciation of all striving for power and a return to nature, an alternative philosophy developed, transforming the past into an ideal as the way to salvation and advocating a return to the old ethical standards. Confucius became its spiritual leader.

Like the early Chinese rulers, he believed that human society, from the most powerful ruler to the lowliest peasant, was part of an all-embracing eternal cosmic order. In this structure everything had its ordained role, which had to be adhered to for the sake of stability. Because everything that happened in the cosmos was governed by an essentially moral force, morality as a rule of conduct must also determine human behaviour.

Not that Confucius saw the chaos surrounding him – the rulers' thirst for power, the abuse of office by the state bureaucrats, the selfishness of individuals – as a reason to incite revolution. He was in no way questioning the feudal structure: on the contrary. For him it was an absolute necessity for the reestablishment of universal order and a stable society. 'Let it be as it always was' – with this credo he appealed to his contemporaries to return to virtues which allow men to coexist in organized harmony: justice, goodness, truth, honour, respect for one's elders.

To safeguard his position a ruler must be the perfect embodiment of these virtues. According to the Confucian ideal he is responsible, as the highest temporal authority, for harmony with the supernatural powers and, as the high priest, for the sacrificial rituals securing the favour of the cosmic forces. If this harmony is disturbed and the country is ravaged by natural disturbances such as floods, drought or epidemics, he has failed and is no longer worthy of his mandate. The business of government, on the other hand, is in the hands of an elite ruling class of educated officials, the mandarins. Only those who pass the most rigorous examinations and so have unchallengeable authority for the political/bureaucratic and spiritual/cultural leadership entrusted to them qualify for this task. If this ruling class lives up to the moral standards required of it and exemplifies them, the state is secure, the welfare of its citizens assured. Confucius did not propose that the population as a whole should have any say. As far as he was concerned they were only required to be honest and obedient.

His high-minded moral theories did nothing to alter the situation. Confucius set up a school at which he trained young men for public service according to his ideas and attracted followers who later ensured that his ideas and speeches were preserved for posterity in writing. Later he travelled from court to court offering his services and advice. But not a single one of the princes heeded his warnings. When he died Confucius was an embittered and lonely man.

It was not until the disputes between small states came to an end in China and a new era of political strength and cultural expansion began with the Han dynasty in the second century BC that Confucian teaching received the recognition that its founder had hoped for in vain during his lifetime. The Han rulers posthumously elevated Confucius to a Revered Sage, made his ideal of cosmic harmony the guiding principle of their own behaviour, his educational and moral standards maxims for the mandarins, his political and moral teachings the code of behaviour for the whole nation.

Despite all the efforts of the Vietnamese to evolve a concept of history from the ancient legends of primal mothers and kings going back to the 3rd millennium BC, there are no reliable accounts of how people lived in the Red River Delta when they were subjugated in 111 BC. Authentic historiography began only with the Chinese occupiers and the writing which they brought with them. According to their records the land was covered with dense jungle, which the peasants burned to clear a space for their rice fields and tilled with stone ploughs. They supplemented cereal growing with hunting and fishing. They lived in village communities, bound together by ancestor and spirit worship. There was no feudal structure as there was in China, but dominant families controlled large areas like princes.

The mandarins sent there, whose first task was to divide the colony into districts and collect taxes, soon set up schools to teach Vietnamese junior administrators the Chinese script and language, familiarize them with Chinese technology and above all indoctrinate them with Chinese culture, thought and Chinese Confucianist values. But they were not so successful as they had hoped in persuading their new subjects to adopt the Chinese way of life. It took a long time for the masses to accept Confucianism, in contrast to Taoism, also brought by the occupiers, whose mystic rituals were much closer to the people's animism, and Buddhism, which began to gain a foothold in Vietnam as an independent religion.

The evolution into a Confucian society was completed only in later centuries of occupation. An educated ruling class developed in the colony, growing generation by generation, and under its influence the people began to incorporate Confucian ideas in their religious life. The traditional ancestor and spirit worship took new forms in the ritual regimentation of the ancestor cult and official religious ceremonies to worship the earthly and heavenly powers.

When the Chinese were finally driven out in 938, after 1049 years of occupation, Confucianism was firmly established in the north of Vietnam. There was a brief period of anarchy in which the

Steles with the names of mandarins on the backs of tortoises in the courtyard of the Temple of Literature, Hanoi

liberation heroes tried to obliterate all memory of the Chinese in the initial euphoria of independence, but the establishment of the Ly dynasty in the 11th century signalled a return to the Chinese master's principles.

A school set up by King Ly Than Tong in the capital Thang Long – later Hanoi – in 1070 to train mandarins to be sent into the countryside as officials and teachers became the centre for what was now the Vietnamese-Confucian national culture. The sole purpose of teaching, based on the Chinese model, was to preserve tradition. The candidates were not required to think for themselves or even to have enquiring minds; they were strictly confined to learning the Confucian political and moral philosophy in five canonical and four classical works. The teaching and examinations were in the Chinese script and language. Those who passed were fitted for the highest office because, according to the master, education is the way to wisdom, it is the only qualification for irreproachable morality. But the Vietnamese were slow to adopt a principle which almost made the traditionalist Confucius a pioneer of democracy: that access to the elite should be open to anyone with the necessary education, regardless of origins or rank. It was nearly two centuries before the names of mandarins from the peasant class also appeared on the steles in the courtyard of the Van Mieu, the Temple of Literature in the capital.

In their rigid adherence to Confucian institutional and ceremonial systems, the rulers of Vietnam for a long time used his ideas not only as a code of behaviour but also as an instrument which always had a stabilizing effect in crises caused by expansionist or internal power struggles. In the 19th century, however, this dogmatism proved a fatal weakness; the Vietnamese emperors were so politically inflexible that they had nothing else with which to counter European imperialism.

In the French colonial period the influence of Confucian values waned, particularly after the new rulers abolished the traditional mandarin examinations in 1918 to prevent the emergence of a new generation of elite educated Vietnamese who might prove nationalistic and rebellious. They did, on the other hand, continue to allow the traditional official spirit-worshipping ceremonies which up to 1945 were still held in Hue, the capital of the Nguyen rulers, on the Nam Giao, the altar of heaven and earth. In the end, however, these were celebrated only by emperors installed by the French as compliant puppets.

It must seem almost illogical that Confucianism became stronger again after the victory of the Socialist revolution. One explanation is that Ho Chi Minh himself and many of his leading comrades still came from the class educated in the Confucian tradition. Many Vietnamese saw him as a reformer, the new executor of the heavenly mandate that had traditionally been given to the rulers. Also, the Confucian code of loyalty which, in contrast to the Western system, always subordinated the rights of the individual to duty to the state, was easily translated into Socialist principles. Although citizens, whatever their personal political views, might not be conscious of them as such, the principles of Kung-fu-tse are still the fabric of Vietnamese society.

Buddhism: spiritual comfort and way to salvation

The records that have been handed down give no definite indication of how Buddhism came to Vietnam and China. The doctrine that had originated in India 500 years earlier probably arrived in both countries simultaneously at the beginning of the Christian era.

An access route opened up with the Silk Road, a trading road on which the Chinese Han rulers had precious goods, mainly silk, porcelain and furs, transported to distant markets. It ran along the edge of the Takla Makan desert to India across the Hindu Kush mountain range, from where many of the goods travelled on via Afghanistan and Persia to Egypt and Rome. The most difficult part of the journey was the desert route. 'No sign of life in the sky, none in the endless waste of sand,' wrote a Chinese chronicler. 'The only landmarks are the bones of those who died here.' But hardship and danger did not deter Indian monks from accompanying the camel caravans returning to China with gold, glassware and woollen goods to carry the message of Buddhism.

Another route lay across the sea. Indian ships, laden with spices and accompanied by Buddhist monks, sailed to Indonesia and then on across the South China Sea towards China, stopping off in Ceylon, now Sri Lanka. Their schedule depended on the monsoon winds. Their destination was Luy Lau, a river port that the Chinese had built as their administrative and trade centre after occupying the north Vietnamese provinces. The city's position was ideal. Shielded from the storms across the open sea but still accessible to trading ships via the

Red River Delta, Luy Lau became a transshipment port for all the goods obtained in the colony by the Han occupiers: wood from the jungles, tiger skins, elephant tusks and raw silk produced from silkworms in mulberry plantations. Businessmen and mandarins were the first to hear of Buddha's teaching from Indian sailors, traders and monks.

Historical facts and dates were not considered important in India at that time and the dates given for the Buddha – 563 to 483 BC – are not all that reliable, but there is no doubt that the founder of the religion actually existed. His father was called Suddhodana and as the head of the Gautama family he was the prince of the Sakya tribe which ruled parts of what is now Nepal. His mother Mayadevi died shortly after her son's birth and he was given the name Siddharta, 'He who achieves his goals'. The story goes that the child began his life with seven steps to the four points of the

Mural of the newborn Sakyamuni in the Pho Minh pagoda, Rach Gia

compass, pointing up with one hand and down with the other – a sign of his future role as an intermediary between heaven and earth. According to another story, nine dragons sprinkled him with water for his first bath. The two stories are often depicted in sculptures and paintings.

Because of his position, the boy could look forward to a life of privilege, power and wealth. Siddharta Gautama married at the age of 17 and his wife Yashodhara bore him a son, Rahula. But soon the young man began to be plagued by doubts and questions about the meaning of life, expressed symbolically in a legend: while out with his coachman Chandaka, Siddharta noticed an old man dragging himself painfully along. 'Why is that old man suffering?' asked the prince's son and his servant answered, 'Because that is the way of the world.' A little while later Siddharta saw a sick man doubled up with pain and a funeral procession accompanied by lamenting relatives and again Chandaka explained to him: 'That, my lord, is man's fate.' But then Siddharta caught sight of a beggar who was not unhappy in spite of his poverty but looked up at him with a cheerful expression. These encounters had a decisive effect on him. The next night he left his pampered life in the palace and his family to set out on the long road that eventually led to his becoming the Sakyamuni, the wise man of the Sakya tribe, and the Buddha, he who has found *bodhi*, enlightenment.

Like China at the same time, where moral decline led to the teachings of Confucius, India was also in a situation which called for a new spiritual direction. The most important feature of its society was the caste system, which assigned people to a rank in society from birth. The upper class were the intellectuals, the brahmans, under them were the warriors, under them the traders, and right at the bottom the toiling masses. The brahmans had sole control over the worship of the gods still found today in the Hindu religion and under their priestly supervision religious life consisted of nothing but formal rituals. The concept of karma and rebirth, the doctrine that man determines his position in the next life by good or bad behaviour, was equally rigid. Under the influence of the priestly caste the way out of this cycle was not through individual behaviour but by unquestioning religious submission.

Siddharta Gautama expounded a different theory, that whatever his rank man can lead an honest life through his own initiative. This in turn enables him to escape his karma, to avoid the painful process of rebirth and finally to reach the status of an Arhat by renouncing all earthly things and reaching Nirvana. The philosophical bases of this doctrine of salvation are the Four Noble Truths which came to the Buddha after six years' fasting and meditation under the bo-tree. With their proclamation he set the 'wheel of teaching' in motion and laid the foundations for the Buddhist religion.

The Buddha preached that suffering is part of human existence. Man's suffering comes not only from old age and illness but also from joy, because when it comes to an end it also causes suffering; suffering is not conquered by death, but comes back to men after rebirth. The reason for the constant repetition of suffering by rebirth is that man is governed by his instincts, his greed for belongings and sensual desires. The only way to escape from this cycle of suffering is by eradicating all intemperate desires. According to the fourth Truth, man can acquire the ability to renounce all wrong behaviour which causes suffering by following the Eightfold Path: right contemplation, by heeding the Four Truths; right thinking, free from lust, cruelty and untruthfulness; right speaking, without lying, slander, profanity and idle talk; right living, not harming other creatures; right endeavours to overcome evil and develop good thoughts; right control of the body, the emotions and the mind; right concentration on the essential with the aid of deep meditation.

Statue of the fasting Buddha in the But Thap pagoda

In the intensive search for meaning that was going on in India at the time, the Buddha offered an alternative with his morally based maxims and the promise of salvation. Instead of just formally obeying the brahmans' rules, the individual was free to work hard and gradually, through his own actions, to temper the fate of endless rebirths and repeated suffering, and eventually to find release from it.

Preaching tirelessly, the Buddha wandered the country for another forty-five years after his enlightenment. Although his words were written down only later, in the sutras, his teaching had already spread across India in his lifetime. When he died at the age of 80 there were already communities of monks in monasteries who helped spread his teachings further. As the number of followers increased, a wealth of legends grew up around him, claiming incredible feats. One describes how he went up to heaven to pass the teachings on to his mother. Another story relates how he took the message of enlightenment to his father shortly before his father's death. Both encounters played an important part later when Buddhism spread to Vietnam and China – this performance of filial duty showed that the traditional ancestor worship also had its place in the new religion.

Soon after the Buddha's death differences emerged among his followers, becoming more marked in the next few centuries. The readiness to submit to rigid self-discipline was waning. In the belief that it was given only to a few to achieve the virtues of the Eightfold Path, more and more Buddhist monks and teachers were looking for expedients which would make it easier for believers to reach their goals. On various councils, the most important convened by the Indian king Ashoka in 244 BC, they argued about different interpretations of the Buddha's message. But they were unable to bridge the gulf that had already opened up. Soon afterwards the religion split into two : Theravada or Hinayana Buddhism (Old or Lesser Vehicle school) and Mahayana Buddhism (Greater Vehicle). Both spread across Asia in their different forms: Theravada in Sri Lanka, Cambodia, Laos, Thailand and Burma; Mahayana in Vietnam, China, Tibet, Nepal, Korea and Mongolia.

Theravada Buddhists still adhere strictly to the original doctrine of the Three Jewels: Buddha, his teachings (*dharma*) and the monks (*sangha*). They revere the historical human teacher, who simply passed on his knowledge of salvation after his own enlightenment and leaves it to the individual to determine his own rebirths through his own actions, thus accepting that achieving perfect Arhat status is not possible for everyone.

The Mahayana Buddhists also venerate the founder of their religion. For them, however, he is only one of countless Buddhas embodying universal wisdom and goodness as supernatural and transcendent beings, who appeared temporarily in human form. The founders of Mahayana argued that the Theravadic concept was aimed only at the salvation of the individual and thus – as the Lesser Vehicle – served selfish ends. They therefore replaced the Arhat ideal with that of a Bodhisattva, a being who had gained access to Nirvana in the course of previous rebirths but had relinquished it to help the defenceless human race in Buddha-like dedication. Mahayana Buddhism promises that anyone can achieve this state of being simply by a willingness to demonstrate religious faith, virtuousness and service to others.

Mahayana Buddhism quickly became popular, particularly with the introduction of the Bodhisattva. The historical Buddha, who had refused deification for himself, faded more and more into the background. Now transcendent, he soon found himself in the company of countless Buddhas and Bodhisattvas, all serving the purpose of making the way of enlightenment easier for believers. In the centre of this pantheon are Amitabha, Sakyamuni and Maitreya, the Buddhas of past, present and future.

The Mahayana teachers appointed Amitabha the prince of a kingdom of salvation, which they described as Pure Land or Western Paradise. Without abolishing the religious objective of Nirvana, the total dissolution of self, which was hard for the masses to understand, they painted a fantastic picture of this paradise as an intermediate state on the way to salvation – filled with celestial music, evergreen trees, sweet-smelling rivers and with the Eternal Light of the Amitabha always near. At his side is the Bodhisattva Avalokiteshvara, often portrayed with a thousand eyes which see all misery and a thousand arms which come to the aid of mankind. In Vietnam he has been made into a female figure, Quan Am, the Goddess of Mercy, probably because of his characteristics of sympathy and compassion which are more commonly associated with women.

Attempting to make the religion comprehensible and at the same time accessible to the masses, Mahayana Buddhism also broke away from the doctrine of Sakyamuni, in which there are no gods and therefore no images of gods. For a long time the Theravada followers portrayed their saviour only in symbols – as a footprint of the Enlightened One, in the form of his wheel of law or symbolized by the lotus blossom growing out of the darkness into purity – whereas the Mahayana altars were filled with statues of Buddhas and Bodhisattvas. More than any religious buildings these figures, cast in bronze, chiselled in stone and carved from wood, with their faces radiating calm and peace, quickly helped Mahayana Buddhism gain the confidence of the population as it spread into Asia.

As with Taoism, which arrived in the north of Vietnam at about the same time, people had no difficulty in integrating the Buddhist religion into their traditional beliefs. Taoism, with its mystical ceremonies, enhanced day-to-day exchanges with the spirits. Buddhism offered people a refuge for the soul. Until then, fear of the forces of nature and the spirits and the need for reconciliation with them had shaped the lives of the hard-working rice farmers. For the first time the new religion gave them hope and comfort. It spoke to them in terms with which they were all too familiar – suffering and pain. The virtues of renunciation that it required were difficult to achieve but the promise of salvation brought them happiness.

An active religious traffic developed straight away. Monks from China and its Vietnamese colony went to India, Indian monks came to meet them. They brought with them in their luggage the doctrine's scriptures, which it took generations of scholars to translate, since there were very few people who could transfer the original Sanskrit texts into Chinese.

One of the travellers influenced the development of Mahayana Buddhism more than anyone else: the Indian monk Bodhidharma, the first patriarch at the beginning of the 6th century and

Statuette of Quan Am, the popular Goddess of Mercy

spiritual head of the Chinese Buddhist community. He founded meditation Buddhism, the Inner Light school, based on the principle that recognition of Buddhist truth and enlightenment is achieved not by striving to interpret and observe the scriptures but by peace and deep contemplation. As Thien Buddhism (Chan in Chinese, Zen in Japanese) this doctrine was also disseminated in Vietnam half a century later, introduced by the Indian scholar Vinitaruci, whose pupil Phap Hien became the first Vietnamese patriarch in 626.

From then on, Vietnamese Buddhism began to merge with other beliefs. The oldest example is the Dau pagoda in the village of Thanh Khuong east of Hanoi. Under its brick roof statues of Buddha and Arhat mingle with the figures of animistic rain and cloud goddesses. There is even a Hindu fertility lingam on the altar, its origins lost in the mists of the country's religious history.

Thien Buddhism now bore very little resemblance to the original Indian form of the doctrine and over the centuries they diverged even more. For many believers meditation was too arduous. Instead, with typically Vietnamese pragmatism, they expressed their longing for comfort and help by calling on the Paradise Buddha Amitabha, A Di Da in Vietnamese. They still do so today. In the

Wall painting and statue of the Mahayana monk
Bodhidharma

pagodas and pilgrim temples, which over the years
have been more and more lavishly and richly decorated with statues, surrounded by the chanting of
the yellow-robed monks and the scent of the ever-
burning incense sticks, they combine worship and
the expectation of help by endlessly repeating his
name in their prayers.

Pagodas and religious art

Linguistic experts are not certain of the derivation
of the word *chua*, first mentioned in the 11th
century, which the Vietnamese use for pagodas and
monasteries. It is believed to originate from the
Pali and Sanskrit words *thupa* and *stupa*. It is also
not clear when the first *chua*s were built. Although
Vietnamese archaeologists have uncovered the
foundations of old temples in the northern
provinces and even now are constantly excavating

new examples of ancient religious art such as stone
altars, steles or decorated bricks, the date of the
first pagodas has not been established. It is believed
that in the early days of Buddhism in Vietnam, its
followers still venerated their new figures of
worship in front of the old spirit altars, usually
under simple straw roofs. The growing number of
followers, the establishment of communities of
monks in monasteries, the visits by scholars
needing accommodation and space for the transla-
tion of the sutras and above all the growth of the
pantheon soon made it necessary to build perma-
nent structures of wood and stone.

Building a new pagoda was an undertaking
which affected the future and happiness of the
whole village, in the same way as a new house did
for the family, and it could not be embarked on
without the advice of experts on the earth,
heavens, spirits and gods. According to a docu-
ment that has been handed down, 'The right place
and the right day for building the temple have to
be carefully chosen; then faith will prosper, the
monks will think clearly and everyone involved in
the building will be blessed.' The builders of the
early pagodas in north Vietnam always sought
harmony with nature. Later sacred buildings too,
whether in the countryside or the towns, are
always adapted to their surroundings. This is
prompted mainly by the religious fear that the
spirits of nature living in the mountains and waters
and in the landscape as a whole will be disturbed
by man's work and refuse their protection.

There was, however, no set style or consistent
design for pagodas and monasteries. The architecture of the *chua*s is as varied as the Vietnamese
landscape with its rice plains, rivers, lakes and
mountains. Money was also a significant factor in
size and decoration, unless the founders were kings
or nobles. In poorer villages pagodas often consist
of just a simple building with the altar, offertory
table and utensils under one roof. Others are
extensive: entrance portals with three gates, separ-

ate bell- and drum-towers, buildings in several sections for combined and separate altars for the Buddhist, Taoist and animist gods, rooms for offerings, side temples, separate accommodation for the monks, gardens and surrounding walls. In the 10th to 13th centuries many pagodas also had a *thap*, a square or round tower several storeys high to honour a patriarch or house relics. Only a few renovated examples have survived. Smaller stupas too are still common today as burial places for important monks.

An architectonic feature common to all *chua*s in north Vietnam is the use of wooden supports. The later heavy brick roofs with their often elegant upsweeping corner buttresses are based on a timber frame structure, set on wooden pillars, like the vertical wooden pillars which used to support the light straw roof of the temple huts. Walls, whether they are made of wood or burnt clay bricks, are not for support; they simply provide protection against the weather. There are no intermediate levels and no windows in the wall between the floor and the roof ridge, making the offering and altar rooms dark and solemn but at the same time airy and lofty.

The rapid spread of *chua*s – hundreds of pagodas were built in the reign of the Ly kings from the 11th to the 13th century alone – created innumerable opportunities for craftsmen and artists. Woodcarving, ceramics, stonework, bronze casting and lacquer work flourished. Many works were destroyed at the beginning of the 15th century when a Chinese attack unleashed a new war of liberation, but much of the old stonemasons' work survived – for instance, the life-size animal sculptures and the statue of Buddha in the Pat Thich pagoda, smashed but later restored, or the dragon-shaped staircase balustrade at the temple of Co Loa.

The art of woodcarving was particularly flourishing, thanks to the characteristic wooden structure of the north Vietnamese sacred buildings and the growing need for altar figures. Many of the roof beams and panels in the pagodas are decorated with the works of unknown masters. They show religious figures, scenes from legends, fabulous beings or animals such as dragons, phoenixes, unicorns, tortoises, symbolizing wisdom and longevity in Vietnamese popular belief. The statues of Buddhas, Bodhisattvas and deities dating from the 15th to 18th centuries are particularly fine. Many were made of a mixture of lime, sand, ground shells and paper pulp with sugar cane juice as a binding agent; this could be modelled into unusually smooth and soft statues. Most, however, are made of wood. Artists found a variety of woods of different textures and colours in the forests of Vietnam at the time, although these were later destroyed in the uncontrolled forest clearance. Working with lacquer artists, they produced extraordinarily life-like multicoloured wooden sculptures. A classic example is the figure of Avalokiteshvara in the But Thap pagoda, made in 1656; its thousand arms and thousand eyes embedded in the palms of the hands seem to move with every beam of light falling on the semi-darkness of the altar room.

Much of the austerity and solemnity of pagoda architecture and art have survived in the north of Vietnam until modern times, but in the south,

Stone dragons on a balustrade in Co Loa

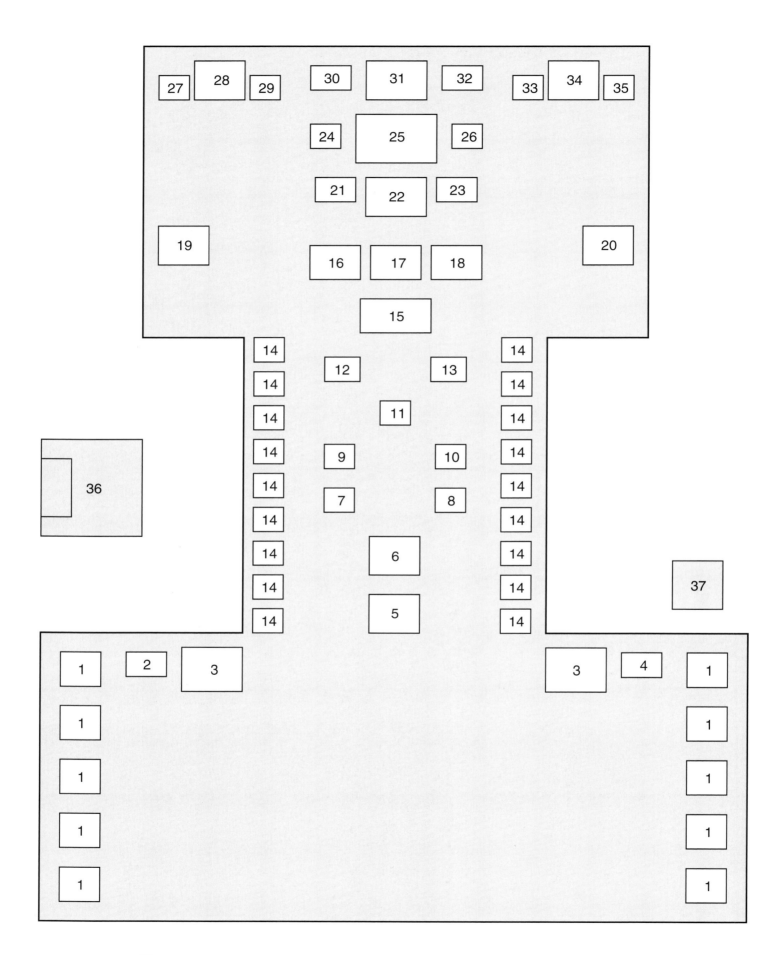

The broad pantheon of the North Vietnamese pagodas

The *chuas* contain a variety of figures of worship representing every shade of religious belief, sometimes several under one roof.

Some pagodas have over a hundred on their altars, occasionally even two hundred or more. This key, from the French historian Louis Bazacier, shows the positions in which the sacred images are found in many pagodas.

ENTRANCE HALL

1   Ten Kings of Hell who watch over the punishment of sinful souls in ten underworlds
2   The earth spirit Tho Dia, who protects the pagoda site
3   Two Dvarapalas, guardians of Buddhist teaching, seated on fabulous beasts
4   The kitchen god Giam Chai, who watches over the offerings brought by the faithful

HALL OF INCENSE

5   Table with a bronze kettle and a wooden gong beaten by nuns and monks at prayer and other utensils
6   Offertory table, usually painted red and gold, with incense containers, flower vases and dishes for offerings and donations
7-10   Four Bodhisattvas, rulers of the four points of the compass
11   The newborn Sakyamuni Buddha, usually surrounded with nine dragons flying in the clouds; one hand points, the other down, symbolizing his future role as an intermediary between heaven and earth
12-13   Brahma and Indra, gods derived from Indian Hinduism who protected the Buddha before his enlightenment. Brahma is sometimes replaced by the Taoist Jade Emperor and Indra by the King of Heaven
14   Eighteen Arhats, saints who have completed the cycle of rebirth

MAIN ALTAR ROOM

15   The dying Sakyamuni Buddha, lying on his side with half-closed eyes and his head propped on his right hand
16   Samantabhadra, a Bodhisattva mounted on a white elephant, embodying wisdom and the law of Buddhist teaching

17   Maitreya, the Buddha of the future, with a smiling face and fat stomach, often surrounded by children
18   Manjusri, a Bodhisattva sitting on a blue lion, holding in his right hand the sword that cuts through doubt and in his left hand the book of the Truths resting on a lotus blossom
19   Bodhidharma, an Indian monk who founded meditation Buddhism, recognizable by his black beard and bushy eyebrows
20   Kshitigarbha, a Bodhisattva shown in the lotus position, who protects penitent souls from the torments of hell
21   Ananda, the Buddha's favourite pupil, whose excellent memory enabled him to record the Enlightened One's teachings
22   Sakyamuni, the historic Buddha as Buddha of the present, often shown with an emaciated body as the fasting Buddha
23   Kaspaya, a Bodhisattva, as an ascetic in simple clothing with his hands folded in front of him
24   Mahasthamaprapta, a Bodhisattva who watches over the respect children show for their parents
25   Amitabha, the Buddha of the past and ruler over the paradise of the Pure Land; venerated by the Vietnamese as A Di Da
26   Avalokiteshvara, a Bodhisattva revered in Vietnam as the female Quan Am, often shown with a thousand arms and a thousand eyes
27   Ba La Mon, helper to the Bodhisattva Ananda, usually white or pink in colour
28   Ananda
29   Tieu Dien, helper to Ananda, mostly painted black or blue
30-32   Amitabha, Sakyamuni and Maitreya as the Three Jewels in the place of honour in the altar room
33   Ngoc Nu, Jade Daughter and helper to the Goddess of Mercy, Quan Am
34   Quan Am, the bestower of fertility, holding a child
35   Kim Dong, known as the Golden Child and, as bringer of good luck, a revered helper to Quan Am

OUTSIDE THE PAGODA

36   Temple known as a *dien*, dedicated to the holy mothers watched over by five tigers
37   Altar known as a *hau*, at which offerings are made for the souls of those who have died without family

Monk on horseback in a wood carving in the Boi Khe *chua*

after the empire and Buddhism spread to the Mekong Delta, it gradually died out. Artistic woodcarvings are rare; instead, the inside wall of the pagodas is often decorated with large paintings, mostly showing scenes from the life of the Buddha. The main building material is stone rather than wood. The building style is often strongly influenced by the Khmer, who used to live in that region: higher buildings with painted or mosaic gable fronts, ridged roofs on several levels, with coloured glazed bricks and the edges of the ridges ending in upsweeping stylized snakes' heads.

Pagoda in the Mekong Delta influenced by the Khmer style of architecture

The variety of religions in the northern pantheon is also less often reflected in the southern *chua*s. The figures on the altars are mainly Buddhas and Bodhisattvas, influenced by the Theravada Buddhism of the neighbouring countries of Laos, Cambodia and Thailand – again without the gravity and depth of the north but often enlarged to a gigantic size and brightly painted.

The community house: shrine for the village's guardian spirit

The Vietnamese landscape and social structure are being altered at a rapid rate by the increase in road transport, road and bridge building, industrial development and the expansion of towns, which act like a magnet. Most villages have electricity, television and refrigerators. But 75 per cent of the population – 95 per cent at the beginning of this century – still live on the land and the way of life of the remote villages has barely changed – small worlds surrounded by a sea of rice fields, the colours varying in the unending cycle of seasons from the moist brown before sowing to the brilliant green of the sprouting stalks and the rich golden yellow of the ripe ears.

The rulers of Vietnam, from the founder kings to the emperors in this century, always abided by the old maxim that 'the government's authority ends at the boundaries of the village'. Each village was surrounded by dense bamboo or cactus hedges or the brick walls often still found in the north, with the houses clustered together behind them. A gate made of wooden pillars with a straw or brick roof, closed at night, was the main access point. Behind it, usually under a spreading banyan tree, narrow lanes led to the different parts of the village. The widest led to the *dinh*, the community house. Even the smaller, poorer villages that could not afford their own pagoda all had their *dinh*. As the centre of community life it symbolized autonomy, as a religious shrine it housed the village's guardian spirit.

The *dinh* is the only traditional and sacred building in Vietnam to which the architectonic principle of harmony with nature does not apply. Often on a monumental scale, with sides sometimes measuring 30 by 20 metres, it is the biggest and most imposing building in the village. Its deep and heavy brick roof, supported on massive wooden pillars, towers over the village huts and dominates them majestically.

The historical origins of the *dinh*s as community houses are not clear. Buildings with roofs showing the upturned corners typical of the *dinh* appear in the reliefs on the bronze drums of the Dong Son culture, dating back 3,000 years or so, named after the place where they were found in the province of Thanh Noa south of Hanoi. Such buildings were unknown in China although they were found in Indonesian-Melanesian culture, used as 'men's houses', meeting places for the village elders.

The oldest *dinh*s still surviving in the typical form date from the 15th century. The right to build a *dinh* was granted by the king, who also gave the place its name and confirmed the guardian spirit chosen by the villages in a certificate. In many *dinh*s these ancient documents bearing the ruler's seal are still preserved as a treasure. It is often difficult to establish what criteria were used to select the *thanh hoang*, the guardian spirit. They are frequently figures from legends or historical figures such as war heroes and famous scholars, founders of villages or particularly respected ancestors, sometimes also feared and therefore venerated animals such as tigers or snakes. Other seemingly unworthy beings also became protective spirits, however: beggars, thieves, people who committed incest and even murderers. The villagers elevated them to the status of guardian spirits in the hope of protecting themselves from the snares of the accursed souls.

The *dinh*s are all equally important. The *thanh hoang* altar is the supreme shrine in the village. As

Tang Lung *dinh* near Hanoi, in need of renovation

the individual families worship at the ancestors' shrine, so the whole village community identifies itself with history in worshipping its protective spirit. Occasionally in the form of a statue but mostly symbolized by a dragon seat, a crown, a festive costume, a silk cloth embroidered with dragons or a weapon, it is kept in the *dinh* in a special room. Under the same roof, wearing blue or black silk robes, the village notables – and in some communities this still happens – took all the important decisions for the community, they informed it of all the events in village life, wed-

Certificate with the seal of the Emperor Minh Mang issued in 1831 for the Xuan Duong *dinh*, Hue

Carving and roof decoration in the Co Loa *dinh*

dings, births, 'news of a sad event' (the death of an inhabitant) or the election of a new councillor elevated to the position by virtue of his age. All high-ranking visitors also used to be received in front of the *dinh* and commended to the protection of the village spirit.

Access to the consecrated room was reserved for men and for boys who had been presented to the village spirit at the age of seven in an official ceremony and were listed as sons of the village. Women were only allowed to go to the square in front of the *dinh* for festivities associated with the

Villagers performing a play for the tiger spirit, around 1939

offering rituals for the guardian spirit, the prayer ceremonies before the rice was sown and thanks-giving festivals after the harvest, mostly combined with markets, popular entertainment, feasting and dancing.

The *hem* festivals organized annually before the beginning of spring but now very rare were particularly lively and colourful. The centrepiece was a play acted by all the villagers, tailored to the story of their particular guardian spirit. If, for instance, the spirit was a blind beggar who had died in tragic circumstances, the circumstances of his death were enacted in melodramatic form. If he was a general, a battle was acted out, often rough and even bloody; the guardian spirit hero was of course the victor. If he was a tiger he was played by a villager in a tiger mask, who hid under the altar in the *dinh*, then jumped out and looked for a victim among the shrieking audience. Whoever satisfied the tiger spirit's bloodlust could begin the feasting and copious quantities of *ruou de* (rice spirit) were drunk.

The central role of the *dinh* in the traditions and administration of the village over the centuries is reflected not only in the impressive solidity of its exterior but also in the often artistic internal decoration. Skilful woodcarvings decorate the entrances to the guardian spirits' shrines, the altars and the roof beams resting on soaring solid wood pillars. Not bound by the religious conventions of pagoda art, many of the panels in the community houses depict the everyday life of the village and its people – fishing and hunting, water buffaloes drawing ploughs, portraits of male and female peasants. Much of this work was not discovered until the 1960s, when Vietnamese scientists first took a closer look at village art. High up under the roof ridges of some *dinhs* they found timber frame reliefs, some unfortunately badly eaten away. This suggested that the unknown carvers had created clandestine works here in secret which the village notables commissioning their work would not have allowed: naked girls bathing, entwined couples, men carousing – clear evidence that the Vietnamese can be cheerful and high-spirited even when living lives of privation.

The heroes' temple: pride in freedom and history

Once upon a time, long, long ago, the dragon king Lac Long Quan, ruler of the seas, met the fairy Au Co, goddess of the mountains. They pleased each other and became a couple and Au Co produced a hundred eggs from which a hundred sons emerged seven days later. But soon afterwards the dragon king left his wife to return to his world. It was only when the mother had brought her sons up to become fine young men that the parents met again. 'You left me alone with our sons and I am living like a widow,' the mountain fairy complained. The water king replied, 'Although our children came from the joining of sea and land, we are like yin and yang, opposites like water and fire, and we are not meant for each other.' So they parted. The dragon prince took fifty of the sons with him to rule over seas and rivers in the future. Au Co returned to the mountains with the other 50 sons, the eldest of whom became king and founded the country's first ruling dynasty under the name Huong Vuong.

Every child in Vietnam knows this fairy story, which is handed down from generation to generation and originated in the rice farmers' early historical legends. Not only does it symbolize the country's culture, ruled since early times by the conflicting elements earth and water, it is also the origin of a cult which influenced Vietnamese religious life as enduringly as all the other religious beliefs – the worship of heroes and heroines. Au Co, the primal mother, is the first of a collection of heroes which developed over the centuries into a whole pantheon of legendary and historic deities.

They are all worshipped in *dens*, temples spe-

cially built for them, externally often similar to pagodas but internally very different. The altar of a *den* contains not the comforting and protective gods from the next world found in the *chua*, Buddhas or Bodhisattvas, Jade Emperors or princes of hell, but earthly founders of empires and victors in battles, martyrs and healers, poets, artists, doctors and scholars elevated to the status of gods. Not all are worshipped all over the country, many have regional or even just local significance. That does not make them any less important in religious life. Whether they are nationally known or just the distinguished scions of a village, as saints they are all on the same high pedestal. Like the pagodas of the heavenly gods, the temples of these earthly gods are always full of incense, their altars full of offerings. And believers pray to the hero figures in the *den* for help, advice and peace of mind in the same way as they do the statues in the *chua*.

The worship of heroes stems from Vietnam's history, the unending succession of occupations and liberations, beginning with subjugation by the Chinese and continuing into modern times with the French and America's military policy. Each foreign occupation merely strengthened the longing for independence, each division the sense

Altar for Au Co, the primal mother, in the Hang Kenh *dinh*, Haiphong

of national cohesion, each humiliation the people's pride in their own achievements.

That also explains why freedom fighters are especially glorified and are first in the hierarchy of heroes. Right at the top are the sisters Trung Trac and Trung Nhi who led a revolt against the Chinese in 40 AD, gathered an army around them, liberated parts of the colonized north and proclaimed themselves queens. When they were overpowered by a stronger Chinese army after reigning for only two years, instead of submitting to further repression they threw themselves into the Hat Giang river. Their pride and patriotism are an example to the Vietnamese to this day. During the Vietnam war Ho Chi Minh had ceremonies held for the Trung sisters in their *den* to identify his guerilla war against the south (allied with the U.S.) with the nationalist rebellion of the heroines and to mobilize women for the struggle.

The most illustrious of the male heroes in this category is the military leader Ngo Quyen, who gained a victory over the Chinese and ended their colonial rule through his strategy in 938. Under cover of night he had wooden piles driven into the river bed not far from the mouth of the Dang. When the high tide washed over the iron-covered tips of the piles, he lured the Chinese fleet into the river with his soldiers rowing light boats and apparently easy to defeat. As the river started to ebb, the heavy war junks of the Chinese became stuck, helplessly vulnerable to the *coup de grâce* by Ngo Quyen and his troops.

Later occupying forces failed to learn from this defeat. When the armies of the Mongol Kublai Khan invaded Vietnam 350 years later, the king's son was able to halt the enemy on the same river, using the same trick. His tactic of avoiding an open battle and instead cutting off the enemy's supply routes, luring its units into traps and harassing it in mainly nocturnal attacks wore the Mongols down until they abandoned their campaign.

This kind of underground fighting was brought

Bust of Ho Chi Minh in the Phu Ung hero temple, Hanoi

to a fine art by the Vietnamese general Le Loi when the Chinese tried again to annex their little neighbour to the south at the beginning of the 15th century. He gathered farmers from every village around him; operating in small groups of partisans and attacking mainly at night, they made skilful use of their familiarity with the swamp and jungle habitat. The Chinese, although militarily stronger, had to capitulate after two decades – a successful resistance strategy which was also used against the French and the Americans five hundred years later. Unlike his well-equipped Western opponents, General Vo Nguyen Giap, the military leader on the Ho Chi Minh side, had studied the underground war waged by Tran Hung Dao and Le Loi very carefully. The two heroes are still remembered in *dens* and street names as if they had fought in the most recent liberation wars.

The kings of the early Vietnamese dynasties

were also revered as heroes throughout the country. The oldest of the temples dedicated to them were built at their former seats: for the legendary Hung kings in the mountains near the city of Viet Tri north-west of Hanoi, to which hundreds of thousands of pilgrims come in April each year for the feast of the ancestors, lasting for several days; for the Hung successor An Duong Vuong, who united the Au and Lac tribes in the Au Lac empire two centuries before Christ, in his former capital Co Loa, where in the last few decades archaeologists have uncovered the old ramparts; for King Dinh Tien Hoang, whose first *den*, later frequently rebuilt, was built in Hoa Lu in the 11th century, his citadel surrounded by limestone rocks. Even today hordes of visitors with incense and prayers pay their respects to the king's statue and the sculptures of his three sons every spring.

The fact that the removal of kings and changes of dynasty were often accompanied by bloody fighting, internal unrest and suffering for the peasants does not make the heroes any less important as symbols of national independence. The reverence paid to them in the numerous *dens* built for them later is not only for the individual kings but also for their companions, descendants, women, mandarins and soldiers. The resistance against the French colonial rulers also produced many heroes, all of whom symbolize Vietnamese ideals and virtues – public order, national pride, self-sacrifice. The tradition of hero worship still continues: Uncle Ho, the father of modern Vietnam, now has a place on the altar in many *dens*.

Another category of *den* is dedicated to heroes who did not win their laurels in battle or belong to dynasties but were often legendary benefactors who used their superhuman power for the good of the people. A classic example is the mighty Tran Vu, the king of heaven's general, who rid the inhabitants of the Red River Delta of a nine-tailed fox. The monster, so the story goes, struck terror into the inhabitants of the forests where Hanoi

Temple for victims of the resistance against the French colonial government, Hue

now stands. He ate women and children, until the king of heaven heard the entreaties of the frightened people. Tran Vu fought the monster for many days. In the fight, a deep depression was trodden in the damp earth and from it sprang the biggest stretch of water in the capital, the West Lake. Near its bank the grateful peasants built a *den* for Tran Vu. With its black bronze statue four metres high and weighing four tons, the biggest in Vietnam, the temple attracts many visitors even today from far and near.

There are countless *dens*, often quite modest, dedicated to minor local popular heroes, such as the son of a village who became a scholar, a craftsman or an artist who created something special in his field. Truong Trung Ai for example, who in the 3rd century introduced the use of the potter's wheel, learned from a Chinaman, to his village Dau Khe; Tue Tinh, who became the first doctor in his village Van Thai in the 10th century; Tran Truong Cong, who passed on the art of lacquer painting to his village Binh Vong in the 15th century; Phung Khac Khoan, who introduced corn- and soya-growing to his village Phung Xa in the 16th century. Their names are not in the history books but they, like thousands of others, are the pride of their village community. Just as the pilgrimages and state ceremonies for the major national heroes unite the whole nation, the local heroes unite the villages in the *rang to tien*, the communal duty to give thanks to the revered dead, who even now are repaid with religious devotion.

The Chinese pantheon: enhancement of popular religion

Although the beliefs imported into Vietnam were the result of the Chinese occupation, neither the people nor the aristocracy ever saw them as imposed. When the occupation ended 1,000 years later, Taoism and Buddhism were for a long time inseparable components of popular religion, the teachings of Confucius remained for many years the basic principles of political and social order in Vietnam.

Like the kings of the first enduring line of rulers, the Ly dynasty which reigned from 1010 to 1225, later dynasties right into this century also followed Confucian principles. At the same time, they were usually also devout Buddhists, bringing educated monks to their courts as advisers, encouraging the building of pagodas and giving generous donations of land to the monasteries. At certain times Confucians and Buddhists jealously tried to oust each other from the advisory role at court and the Buddhist influence temporarily declined, but the doctrine of enlightenment lost none of its importance in the country's religious life. On the contrary, since Confucianism was more concerned with order in this life it was always more important to the rulers when the country was unsettled by wars or internal unrest. It was at these times in particular that the people were more inclined to turn to the figures of gods in the temples and pagodas for help.

Vietnam has never had religious wars. When Vietnamese feudal lords extended their rule to the south in the 16th and 17th centuries and took the Hindu kingdom of Cham in the centre of the present country, these were wars of conquest and not religious wars. Hinduism had been the state religion there for thousands of years, with intervals of Buddhism. The Cham kings saw themselves as incarnations of the Hindu god Shiva; the deities worshipped were Vishnu, Indra, Brahma, the elephant-headed Ganesha and the lingam and yoni fertility symbols. But it was not because of religion that the empire was destroyed; it was a bulwark against any further advance to the south, down to the fertile Mekong Delta, until then ruled by Khmer kings.

Hinduism disappeared from Vietnam with the Cham empire. But many of the sacred buildings survived as stone monuments to the culture and religion that flourished at the time. Even today the imposing temples, usually with three towers, soar above the hills of central Vietnam. They are all respected as holy places and historical monuments. The temple of the Cham goddess in Nha Trang in particular attracts many visitors.

After the territorial expansion of the Vietnamese state as far as the mouth of the Mekong at the end of the 18th century, tens of thousands of Chinese immigrants arrived in the country. Some stopped halfway in Hue, which soon afterwards became the new capital of the Nguyen emperors. But most settled on the outskirts of Saigon, at that time relatively insignificant, and founded Cholon, which soon became and remained one of the liveliest districts in the developing metropolis. Not only did the Chinese bring craftsmanship and an enthusiasm for trade, they also had an extraordinarily active community and religious life. Even in the early years they built many *hoi quan*, temples, which were also used as meeting places. Most of them escaped the subsequent wars and still survive.

These Chinese religious buildings, often known as pagodas, are easily recognizable from the outside by their glazed brick roofs, their fantastic dragon decorations on the roof beams and internal pillars, their colourful ceramic friezes usually depicting crowds of people in Chinese village scenes and the long spirals of incense strung on wires, glowing in the open inner courtyards. In their sanctuaries Taoist figures predominate: the goddess Thien Hau for example, the patroness of sailors, with her two servants Thien Ly Nhan (thousand mile eyes) and Thuan Phong Nhi (good winds ears); the red-faced Quan Cong with his red horse Zich Tho who brings good luck, originating from the legendary general of the Chinese Han dynasty and revered in particular as the protective god of travellers; or Than Tai, the bringer of happiness and prosperity, usually dressed in white. The cult of mothers and fertility goddesses is even more important than in the Vietnamese pagodas; young women and couples wanting children pray in front of their statues in particular.

Although the Chinese mixed little with the Vietnamese and Cholon is still the Chinatown of Ho Chi Minh city, the immigrants' temples were never seen as alien from the cultural or religious point of view. In spite of or precisely because of the characteristics of the Chinese pantheon, many

Lingam (a Hindu fertility symbol) in the Dau pagoda

Vietnamese actually see them as an enhancement of their own traditional religious beliefs.

The extremes which Vietnamese religious flexibility allows are demonstrated by a sect founded in 1925 which managed to combine all the components of Asian and European religions and others: the movement of Cao Dai, the supreme creator. Its saints include Confucius, Lao-tse, Buddha, Jesus Christ and John the Baptist. It incorporates both ancestor worship and spiritualism; earthly figures such as Lenin, Churchill, Joan of Arc or Louis Pasteur are also worshipped, under the sign of an eye watching over the world.

The headquarters of the sect, run on Catholic lines with a pope, cardinals and bishops, is a cathedral in Tay Ninh, north-west of Saigon, whose gaudily coloured decorations are as exaggerated as its synthesis of philosophies. Miniature versions of this building, with its two towers, are found in many villages and towns in the south of Vietnam. Members pray there four times a day. But Caodaism has never managed to attract more than two million followers. Its strict hierarchy and rituals were too alien to the Vietnamese population for it to be a substitute for the popular religion which allows everyone total freedom of belief and interpretation.

Vietnam does, however, have a relatively large Christian community. No precise figures are available but it is estimated at five per cent of the population, around four million people. The towers of Catholic churches, nowadays often in a state of disrepair, are found all over the country, but Catholicism never merged with the popular religion. If there was ever any chance of that happening it was ruled out when the missionaries who came to the country in large numbers in the 19th century required converts to Christianity to profess the Christian faith exclusively and renounce all their old traditions, gods and spirits. For most of the population this was out of the question.

Bloody conflict ensued when the emperors of the Nguyen dynasty tried to curb the proselytizing zeal of the Christian missionaries, driving them out of the country and, when this did not work, having some of them killed. The 'colonial forces' then sent from France heralded French colonial rule. From then on Vietnamese Catholics also played an important political role, particularly when the Americans appointed Catholic governors in South Vietnam after the French were driven out. Their efforts to impose Catholicism over the popular religion led to mass protests headed by Buddhist priests. This religious struggle reached its climax in the 1960s when the government banned pagoda festivals and ordered the police to fire on demonstrators in Hue. The monks responded to these acts of violence with violent but spectacular resistance – self-immolation, with the shocking pictures seen all over the world. This was the beginning of the end of American dominance in South Vietnam and at the same time confirmed the separation between popular religion and Catholicism which has persisted to this day.

However, the political activities of the men in the yellow robes were not forgotten even after 1975, when Ho Chi Minh's army of liberation was victorious throughout the country. For his heirs in the Socialist government, the monks remained an unpredictable force, most easily controlled by isolating them from the population at large. It took ten long years for them to realize that Socialism was no substitute for traditions, that with their policy of religious repression they were depriving the starving people of a vital escape valve. 'A stream whose source is blocked will dry up; a tree deprived of its roots will wither' – it was not until the rulers in Hanoi called to mind these words by their leader Ho Chi Minh and with *doi moi*, political and economic liberalization, once again allowed religious freedom that it became clear how much the people had been yearning for it.

Reconstruction: state programme and individual initiatives

In the wide forecourt of the Lan pagoda in Hanoi is a heap of massive tree trunks which will soon be supporting the roof of the altar room; in front of the Pho Minh *chua* in the village of Tuc Mac workmen are levering up a stone tortoise weighing several tons with wooden stakes to pour in new foundations underneath it; next to the Tam Thai pagoda in the Marble Mountains near Da Nang craftsmen are hammering wood into a basin shape to pour in new concrete supporting pillars; in the Go *chua* in Saigon monks are wielding paintbrushes and giving altars and statues a new coat of coloured paint. Snapshots from the spring of 1996 – and just some of the countless examples of the enthusiastic restoration work which is going on at *chua*s, *dinh*s and *den*s all over the country.

Not everyone is in such a happy position as the renovation committee for the Lang *chua*. Not only have wealthy members of the community donated enough money to buy pillars of rare and expensive hardwood but, because the pagoda is one of the

Self-immolation by the monk Thich Quang Duc in Saigon on 11 June 1963

oldest in Hanoi, it is also on a list of sacred buildings whose preservation is being subsidized by the government. Experts from the Ministry of Culture supervise the renovation work and make sure that it does not spoil the architecture and furnishings.

None of the oldest pagodas built in the north of Vietnam in the period of the Chinese occupation, i.e. before the 10th century, survives in its original form. Many were damaged in wars and later rebuilt in a different form. Others were rebuilt or extended with the help of royal donations. Sometimes a village community which had become prosperous simply tore down a modest pagoda and replaced it with a more magnificent building. But the main reason why the pagodas, temples and community houses constantly needed renovating was the perpetually humid climate, which destroyed the wood traditionally used as a building material.

Pagoda near Da Nang surrounded by typhoon floods

Repairing a Bodhisattva statue

War and the climate have ruined countless older and more recent shrines even in this century. For decades they could not be rebuilt because of a shortage of money and ideological objections to religion. But all that has now changed. Delegations of archaeologists, historians and financial administrators have made a survey, drawn up restoration programmes and started to put them into practice. Professors from art schools and their students are at work repairing damaged sculptures. And all over the country, where the arm of the government is not long enough for supervision and subsidies, lay people are setting to work to bring shape and colour back to their religious sites.

The Ministry of Culture has three hundred sacred buildings of historical interest, mainly in the north, on its list so far. But it will probably be years before it is possible to start restoring them all. Until now, the available funds – government subsidies, donations and entrance fees paid by tourists at many sites – have only been enough to maintain and repair a dozen or so. Usually workmen and craftsmen have demonstrated enough care and expertise to satisfy even sceptical experts – at Van Mieu for instance, the Temple of Literature in the centre of Hanoi, where the roofs have been replaced, the heavy beams decorated with artistic

Villagers rebuilding the Cung Chuc *dinh* and the temple façade after renovation

Restoration of roof timbers in the Temple of Literature

carvings and covered with a coat of golden brown paint; at the Phat Tich *chua* in the village of Phuong Oang east of the capital, which was severely damaged in the war against the French and is having a new lobby built in the traditional wooden pillar style, or the Thay pagoda in Sai Son village south-west of Hanoi, where the statues of the Buddhas and Bodhisattvas, protected from the damp under tarpaulins and behind straw mats, are awaiting the renovation of the whole building.

But where money and state control are lacking, individual initiatives and a lack of specialized knowledge often produce less satisfactory results, despite the willingness and enthusiasm. One

example is the Cung Chuc *dinh* in the village of Trung Lap on the Red River Delta plain. This once extensive complex of twenty-five buildings of the 16th century came under French artillery fire in 1949. Only one building survived and the damp has since penetrated through cracks and holes. The beautiful old wood carvings were already badly rotted, stone friezes and steles eaten away by lichen, roof bricks and floor tiles smashed, when the village community – after vainly appealing to Hanoi for help – started restoration themselves at the beginning of 1994. As a pattern for the exterior they used a cloth picture made by a village teacher forty years earlier. Ninety men and women worked for a year and a half, removed the mortar from the old bricks, kept all the old bricks that were still usable, had new roof timbers made and built a new wall more or less the same as the original structure. But inside, very little of the former dignity remained. What used to be wood is now

Two guardian figures in the But Thap pagoda before restoration

... and after

cement; the old brown-painted statues were given garishly coloured robes and crudely painted new faces. The villagers are proud of their achievement; they did their best. But the cultural legacy of Trung Lap has been destroyed.

For concerned experts the uncontrolled use of coloured paint is the most common sin of the self-help restorers. This has happened particularly with many of the newer pagodas in the south, which has always been more lively and colourful. A number of the woodcarvings and sculptures which used to gleam with muted shades of paint have now been repainted in garish colours and the original delicacy of the woodwork has been destroyed with broad brushes and crude strokes. Particularly distressing is the use of multicoloured metallic paints to embellish old altar figures. Although restoration work in the north is generally done with more care, even there, when the work is simply left to the

monks and lay helpers, the old statues are often not restored with the traditional painting but simply covered with gold bronze.

The increasing and often inappropriate use of concrete is also a matter for concern. Understandable as it might be to build cheap cement pillars instead of the more expensive wooden ones, it could be done differently at very little extra cost. During the restoration work on the palaces and temples in the imperial city of Hue a technique has been successfully developed to open up supporting pillars and fill the inside with concrete, then close up the outer layer of wood again and apply the traditional paint. But this technique calls for expert help, which is often not available in the villages.

The electrification of the altars, which is becoming more and more popular, especially in the south, is decorative rather than ceremonial.

49

Hundreds of pagodas, temples and community houses now flicker with coloured light bulbs, neon lights encircle the heads of Buddhas, goddesses, heroes and village guardian spirits. Not even remonstrations from Hanoi have had any effect.

This kind of criticism from intellectual art experts makes very little impression. Just as the religious sites have always reflected the architecture, art, technology and religious beliefs of their time, the modern attributes of our time are simply an expression of the new religious life that is now filling the *chuas*, *dens* and *dinhs* again. What the general public really cares about is the restoration of religious freedom and its musical accompaniment heard all over the country: the sound of the gongs and bells in the pagodas, the chanting of the nuns and monks in the cloisters, the prayers to saints at the altars.

For over 2,000 years the religious faith of the rice farmers survived upheavals, wars and disasters. Kings and emperors, colonial masters and party commissars came and went. It was clear even from Vietnam's early history that decrees by national governments rarely lasted more than a generation. But the gods and spirits of its religion were immortal.

Young woman praying in the Phu Tay Ho den, Hanoi

The Plates:
Religious life in Vietnam, sacred buildings and religious art

Ancient remains: stone altar and overturned steles in the ruins of the Lang pagoda (Minh Hai village, Hai Hung Province)

Buddha statue in the Phat Tich pagoda, probably
11th century, restored with iron clips (Phuong Hoang,
Ha Bac Province)

On the threshold of Nirvana: two Arhat statues in the Bao
Son pagoda (Co Loa, near Hanoi)

Upswept roof corners and carved gable at the Mong Phu
dinh (Duong Lam, Hanoi Province)

PREVIOUS PAGES
Pagoda on Con Son Mountain silhouetted in the grey
morning light (Chi Linh, Hai Hung Province)

60

Homage to legendary kings. A temple festival on Nghia
Linh Mountain (Co Tich, Vinh Phu Province)

Bricks in the shape of mulberry leaves on top of the Chua
Thay pagoda at the foot of the Sai Son Mountains, founded
in the 11th century. In front, a pavilion for water puppet
shows (Thuy Khe, Ha Tay Province).

FOLLOWING PAGES
Holy mothers above a tiger shrine. Taoist altar in the But
Thap pagoda.
The Enlightened One on the lotus throne: Amithaba
Buddha in the But Thap *chua* (Dinh To, Ha Bac Province)

ABOVE AND RIGHT
The stonemason's art under the palm trees. Bell tower at the
But Thap *chua* and animal reliefs on the pagoda balustrade.

FOLLOWING PAGES
The 17th-century Avalokiteshvara with a thousand arms is
regarded as the most beautiful statue in the country. In
Vietnam this Bodhisattva is revered in female form as Quan
Am, the Goddess of Mercy.
Guardian of the newborn Sakyamuni Buddha. A statue of
the Hindu god Brahma in the Tay Phuong pagoda.
In his hands Brahma is holding a mirror, symbolizing
existential nothingness (Thach Xa, Ha Tay Province).

Reflections in the pagoda lake: front building of the 17th
century Keo *chua* (Duy Nhat, Thai Binh Province)

Banana bushes in the pagoda garden: view of the inside of
the Boi Khe *chua* gateway

Dong Lu *dinh* and women washing vegetables in the pool
outside the community house in the early morning mist
(Dong Lu, Ha Tay Province)

Rain under the banyan tree: gate of the 600 year old Boi Khe pagoda (Tam Hung, Ha Tay Province)

The community house, centre of village life and rustic art, in Dinh Bang (Ha Bac Province)

Half-decayed wood relief of a peasant couple, rediscovered
in the roof timbers in the Tay Dong *dinh* (Tay Son, Hanoi
Province)

Altar of the village guardian spirit in the community house,
hidden behind silk embroidery (Tho Ha, Ha Bac Province)

The body of the monk Vu Khac Truong, mummified 300 years ago, behind glass in the Dau *chua* (Nguyen Trai, Ha Tay Province)

Between vegetables and rice: peasant women on the way to market in front of the Thap Binh Son tower (Lap Thach, Vinh Phu Province).

Base of the 900-year-old Thap Binh Son, the oldest pagoda
tower in the country, restored in 1974; behind it the Vinh
Kanh *chua*.

LEFT
Massive pillars on stone bases: front of the Den Dinh, the
memorial temple for King Dinh Tien Hoang, who united
the principalities of North Vietnam in an empire in the
10th century.

The side entrance of the temple for the rulers of the Dinh
dynasty who once had their capital here, with greenery
sprouting from the crevices in the wall (Hoa Lu, Ha Nam
Ninh Province).

The 6th-century Dau *chua*, seat of the first Buddhist patriarch, is the oldest pagoda in Vietnam. The bell tower was built in the 17th century (Thanh Khuong, Ha Bac Province)

Altar for the Rain Goddess Phap Vu, the bestower of fertility, and her helpers in the Dau pagoda

Woodcarving in honour of the divine princess. Peasant
woman drying rice in the courtyard of the Phu Giay *den*,
dedicated to the daughter of the Taoist Jade Emperor. All
the temple towers are decorated with elaborate carvings
(Kim Thai, Ha Nah Ninh Province).

Bright colours in the jungle. One of the most popular destinations for pilgrims is the Perfume Pagoda, which has over a hundred buildings, shrines and grotto temples. The devout are welcomed by a prayer flag on the Trinh *den*, whose roof towers above the trees on the slopes of Ngu Nhac Mountain (Ben Duc, Ha Tay Province)

By the riverside in the morning mist. Pilgrims on their way
to pray at the Thanh Son pagoda, reached by a footpath
from a landing stage.

The Tho Than Mau *dien*, a temple for the Taoist mother goddesses, lies behind a protective wall halfway between the river and the mountains. Behind are the limestone peaks of the Huong Mountains.

Resting place in the monastery garden. The pilgrims' way
leads past the stupa built in the 17th and 18th centuries in
memory of the monks of the Perfume Pagoda

Arrival in the dragon's jaws: 120 steps lead down to the
Huong Tich caves which, according to legend, are the open
mouth of a dragon. In the dark grottos are altars for Buddhist
and Taoist deities. The pilgrims believe that the stalactites
and stalagmites in the vaulted roof also have miraculous
powers. The faithful buy incense and offerings at the stalls.

View from the Thuong *chua*, the highest pagoda in the Bich Dong complex, towards the towering limestone cliffs, shrouded in grey mist. The sun rarely shines on this weird stony landscape (Ninh Hau, Ha Nam Ninh Province).

Effects of the perpetually humid climate. Memorial steles and rotting brick blocks outside the side wall of the Dau *chua* (Nguyen Trai, Ha Tay Province).

A place of honour for the patriarchs. Stupas housing the
ashes of priests from the Tram Gian *chua*. In front, a peasant
girl on the steps to the 12th century pagoda (Tien Phuong,
Hanoi Province)

Tribute to the spirit of the earth. A field shrine surrounded
with eucalyptus trees on the Red River Delta plain (Trung
Am, Haiphong Province).

A grey morning in the north. The Tho Ha pagoda, its size testifying to the village's former prosperity from ceramic making, was damaged in the Indochinese war and is now in ruins (Tho Ha, Ha Bac Province).

FOLLOWING PAGES
Respect for the king of the jungle and his power. The worship of the tiger in Vietnamese popular religion is a mixture of fear and reverence. Shrines and reliefs are dedicated to it as the tutelary spirit of temples and pagodas all over the country

101

Colourful façades in the city centre. The Dau *den* on Hang
Quat, the Street of the Fanmakers, in the old quarter of the
capital Hanoi.

Divine rulers of the elements. Altar of the Taoist holy
mothers in the Dong Quang *chua* in Hanoi. In the top row
Mother Water in white, Mother Sky in red, Mother Forest
in green. The statues in the bottom two rows are their male
and female helpers.

RIGHT
Figure of Mother Water with an embroidered silk robe and
pearl necklace in the *dien* of the Van Ho pagoda in the
south of the capital.

A multitude of gods under one roof. Taoist and hero worship figures side by side in harmony on the two storey altar at the Phu Tay Ho *den* on the West Lake in Hanoi

A little corner among the city wires. The Nhan Noi *dinh*, one of the guardian spirit temples of the old craft guilds (old town, Hanoi)

The Tam Phu *den* in Hanoi, wedged in between shop and house walls. On the gate is a simplified form of the Chinese character for longevity.

111

Seeking a divine general's blessing. Women praying in front of the black-enamelled 4-metre high statue of Tran Vu in the temple named after him on the West Lake in Hanoi. The faithful reverently stroke the feet of the city's legendary guardian spirit.

Washing day at the pagoda. Monks' robes hung up to dry in
the courtyard of the Quang Ba *chua*. Woman washing the
tiles in the forecourt of the Kim Son pagoda (Hanoi).

Worshipping the king's widow. Offertory table and statues
in the Nguyen Phi Y Lan *den*. The memorial temple was
built in the 11th century in honour of Y Lan, who
temporarily ruled the country after the king's death because
his successor was still too young. The colourfully dressed
figures are her female ministers.

On the government's restoration list. The Hang Kenh *dinh*, its heavy brick roof supported by massive pillars. Inside, at the front on the left, is the flower-decorated altar of the village's guardian spirit; at the end of the room an altar to the legendary primal mother Au Co (Le Chan district, Haiphong)

Invoking the spirits in front of the tiger shrine. Wearing ceremonial robes, mediums for the believers gathered around them commune with genies. The woman in red has already gone into a trance at a seance in the Ba Trieu *den* (Phu Dien, Thanh Hoa Province). The woman in white is preparing for the invocation ritual at a similar ceremony in the Dau *den* (Bim Son, Thanh Hoa Province).

FOLLOWING PAGES
The morning after the temple festival. Bundles of burnt out incense sticks, cellophane wrappers from sacrificed rice cakes, faded flowers and fragments of charred money offerings piled up in front of the reliefs of horses and guards at the Cuong *den*, dedicated to the legendary king An Duong Vuong (Dien An, Nghe An Province).

A refuge for animals too. A giant moth alights on a Chinese
wall inscription at Thien Mu pagoda in Hue. A frog basking
in the midday sun on a stone sculpture outside the But Thap
chua.

Midday prayers. A monk in front of the main altar at the
Dieu De *chua* (Hue).

Future preachers of salvation: novice nuns in Dieu Duc
pagoda. They are taught Buddhist philosophy in
Vietnamese, Chinese and English (Hue).

Symbols of living spirit beliefs: flower shrine and family altar
in Hue. Simple offertory tables for the spirits are found all
over the country.

LEFT
Religious figures of the Chinese immigrants. Statue of the
goddess Thien Hau, the patroness of sailors, in Hoi Quan
Ba, the temple and meeting place of a Chinese community.
At the bottom are miniature sculptures of the Goddess of
the Sea and her helpers (Hue).

The best loved figure in popular religion, Quan Am, the
Goddess of Mercy and Compassion, on the altar of the Dong
Thuyen pagoda (Hue). In the Vietnamese pantheon she has
the same significance as the Bodhisattva Avalokiteshvara.

Wisdom and dignity: village elders at the New Year
ceremony (Thon Trieu Son Nam, near Hue).

Victims of the last war. The Xuan Duong *dinh* was hit by a grenade and is now in ruins. The altars of the community house, built in 1831, are also being eaten away by the climate (Hue).

Protected by the coloured dragon: market women outside the Kim Long *dinh*. The inner side of the protective wall outside the community house has a dragon mosaic made of multicoloured porcelain fragments.

Every morning the mendicant monk Khantipala, who
founded the Thien Lam Tu pagoda in 1969, leaves the
pagoda at dawn and walks through a bamboo grove to
receive alms in the surrounding villages (Hue).

FOLLOWING PAGES
Escaping the cycle of suffering and rebirth. This set of small
sculptures is the pride of the Vien Thong pagoda in Hue.
They represent the 18 Arhats who attained salvation in the
Buddhist religion and are on the way to Nirvana. Their joy
is expressed in their faces.

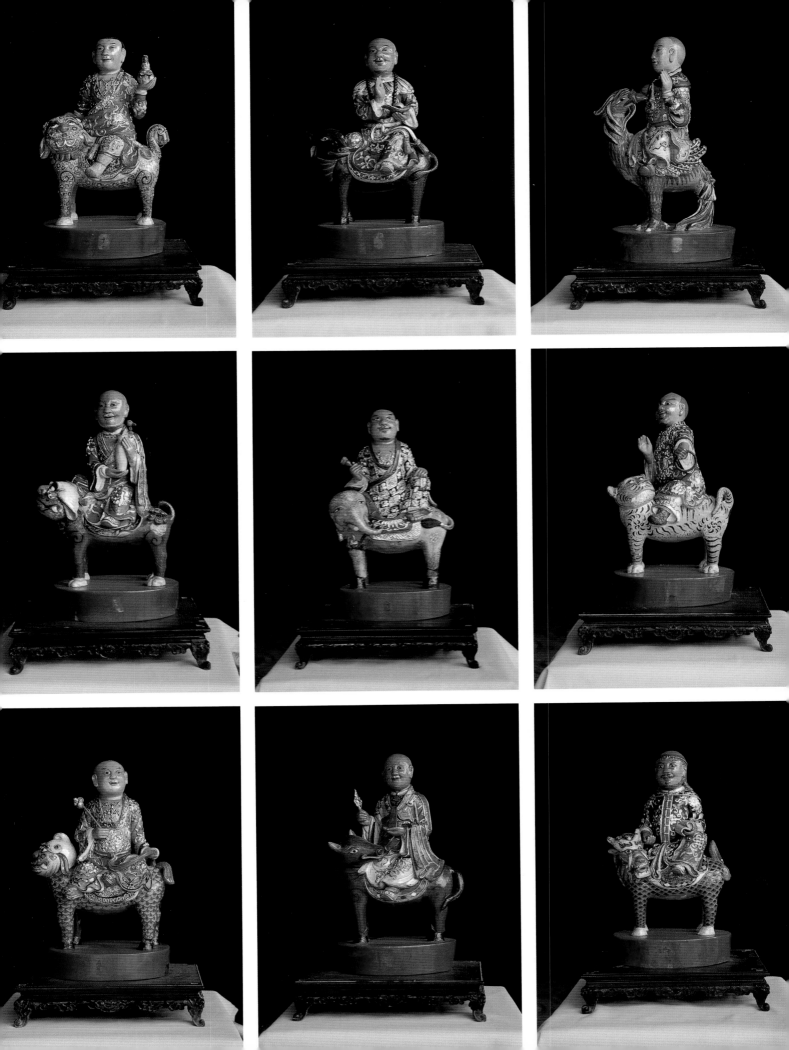

The Enlightened One in a ray of sunlight. The figures of
saints at the grotto temple of Huyen Khong, inside a Marble
Mountain, are in semi-darkness. It is not until midday that
the daylight reaches the Buddha altar in its niche through
an opening in the cave roof (Non Nuoc, Quang Nam-Da
Nang Province).

Group photo outside the village pagoda. Children in front of the Thach Kho *chua* (Xuan Loc, Phu Yen Province).

Stone instead of wood and strong colours. View of the Giao
Hoi *chua* across the forecourt (Hoi An, Quang Nam-Danang
Province). The pagodas and temples in the south of the
country, unlike those in the north, often have colourful
façades and painted cement decoration.

145

Relics of former trade with Japan: lacquered carving in the
Chinese temple of Trieu Chan in Hoi An. The two women
dressed in kimonos have the traditional Japanese hairstyle.
The port was once a maritime trade centre under its former
name of Faifo.

A dull sound from hollow wood: gongs made of wooden
blocks on the altar of the Chuc Thanh *chua* (Hoi An). In all
pagodas and temples nuns and monks play instruments of
this kind as they pray.

Hindu temple towers built by the Cham kings about 900 years ago still tower over the hills of central Vietnam, stone relics of a lost culture. Hinduism disappeared from Vietnam when the Cham empire was destroyed in the 17th century (near Qui Nhon, Binh Dinh Province).

The Po Klaung Garai temple complex, built by the Cham 600 years ago for the gods of the Hindu pantheon, is a monument to a state religion (San, Thuan Hai Province).

Remains of old temple decoration. Only fragments of the hundreds of sculptures that used to adorn the Cham towers survived. Restorers have reconstructed the reliefs of dancers and elephants (Chien Dan, Quang Nam-Da Nang Province).

The all-seeing eye: village temple of the Cao Dai sect (Cam Than, Khanh Hoa Province).

Divine protection for fishing boats. A temple for the
guardian spirit of fishermen, built on a rock in the harbour.
In the background is the Po Nagar Cham temple (Nha
Tang, Khanh Hoa Province).

The Hau Duc pagoda (Nha Trang) nestles among the palm trees.

Roof decoration with the wheel of teaching: Phat Giao Linh
Son pagoda (Nha Trang).

Prayers for peace of mind: service for the dead at the Linh
Son *chua* (Da Lat, Lam Dong Province).

Divine helper: statues of Quan Am, the Goddess of Mercy, in the garden of the Linh Phong pagoda (Da Lat) and outside the Linh Tang *chua* (Di Linh, Lam Dong Province).

The ornate main hall of the Cao Dai sect's cathedral, decorated with coloured dragon pillars. In the centre is the symbol of the eye watching over the world. Priests and adherents gather to pray four times a day (Tay Ninh, Tay Ninh Province).

FOLLOWING PAGES
The island pagoda of Hon Ba, washed by the South China Sea. In front is a shrine to the goddess Quan Am (Vung Tau).

161

164

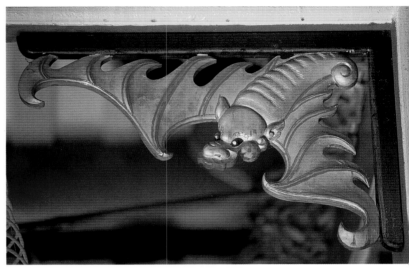

In Vietnamese popular religion bats are believed to bring good luck. They are found in most of the country's religious buildings, in various forms: as a wall relief, a door handle, pillar decoration or carving.

A little China in the south of Vietnam. In the 19th century
Chinese immigrants built numerous temples and meeting
places which – as here at Hoi Quan Thien Hau – they
decorated with coloured miniature scenes from village life in
their homeland and the world of Taoism.

FOLLOWING PAGES
Long spirals of incense hung on bamboo poles or wire above
the open inner courtyards are a typical feature of the
Chinese temples and community houses. The biggest burn
for several weeks.

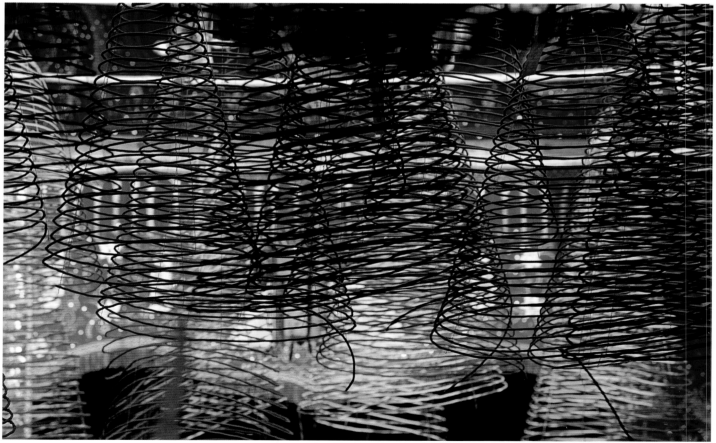

The two Apsaras hanging in front of the Buddhist altar at the An Quang *chua* are a rarity in Vietnamese pagodas. They are more common in other Asian countries, depicted as servants and companions of the gods, dancing or making music.

FOLLOWING PAGES
An electric halo for Amitabha: the main altar at Giac Vien pagoda. As at many other religious sites in Vietnam, the light bulbs and neon lighting are brighter than the old-fashioned oil lamps and candles.

Riding on a fabulous beast: lacquered wood relief with the figure of the Bodhisattva Kshitigarbha on a side altar at the Giac Vien *chua* (Saigon).

171

The supreme ruler in the Taoist pantheon. The Jade
Emperor, flanked by his helpers, on the altar of the Ngoc
Hoang *chua* in Saigon, built by Chinese immigrants in 1909.
The statues are made of lacquered *papier maché*.

NEXT PAGE
The figure of Than Tai, usually – as here in the Ngoc Hoang
pagoda – dressed in white, is particularly popular with
business people. He is believed to repay donations a
thousand times over.

176

PREVIOUS PAGE
A reminder of maternal duty. This figure in a side room at the Ngoc Hoang pagoda, representing a mother who gives way to the temptations of rice wine and neglects her children, is an example of behaviour punished by the gods.

The legendary General Quan Cong, the central figure on the altar of the Phuoc An temple dedicated to him, is venerated equally by the Vietnamese and the Chinese (Saigon).

178

Benevolent red-faced guardian spirit. Statue of Quan Cong with peacock feathers and a coloured headdress at the Hoi Quan Ha Chuong, a meeting hall built by the Chinese in the 19th century.

Mother figures in the Chinese pagoda of Ha Chong,
worshipped especially by women who want children.

Requiem for a father. Children and relatives of a deceased head of the family praying in front of the altar of Lieu Hanh, the Queen of Heaven, in the Quan Am *chua* (Saigon).

RIGHT
Shrine of the dead with photos in the Dai Giac *chua*. If relatives cannot perform the soul rituals themselves, monks are paid to carry out this duty of ancestor worship.

Religious art in lacquer and mother-of-pearl. Intarsia work in the An Quang *chua* (Saigon).

Old glass painting of Quan Am in the Vinh Trang pagoda, in need of restoration (My Tho, Tien Giang Province).

184

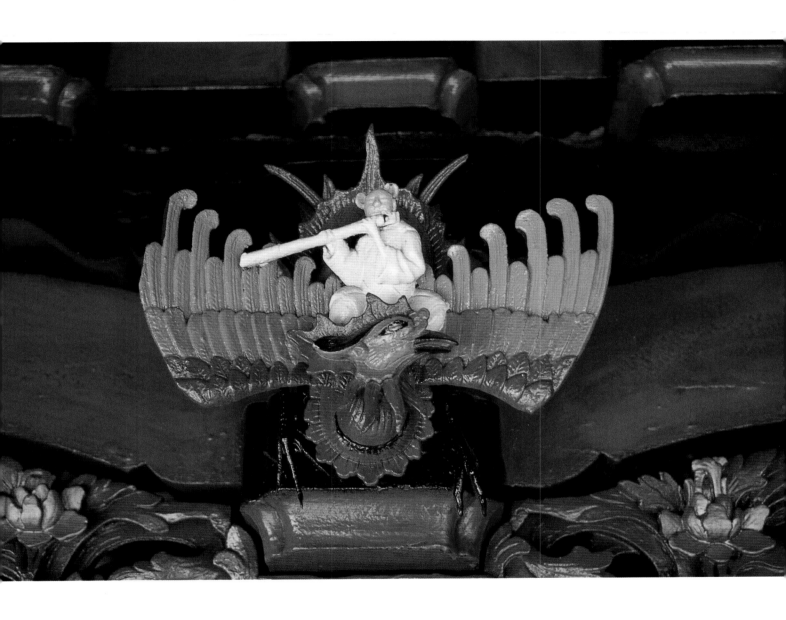

LEFT
Still-life in red: incense container on a lacquered wooden panel in the Giac Vien *chua* (Saigon).

Playing with shapes and colours: flute player on a colourful fantastic bird on the timbers of Hoi Quan Ha Chuong (Saigon).

187

Chinese-style Noah's ark: a gilded carving above the entrance of the Nghia An *chua*. The figures of gods, humans and animals on a junk represent the immigrants' voyage across the sea.

Incense for gods and heroes: incense sticks and candles in the Ha Chuong temple and the *den* for the imperial general Le Van Duyet, who conquered the south of the country in the 19th century (Saigon).

189

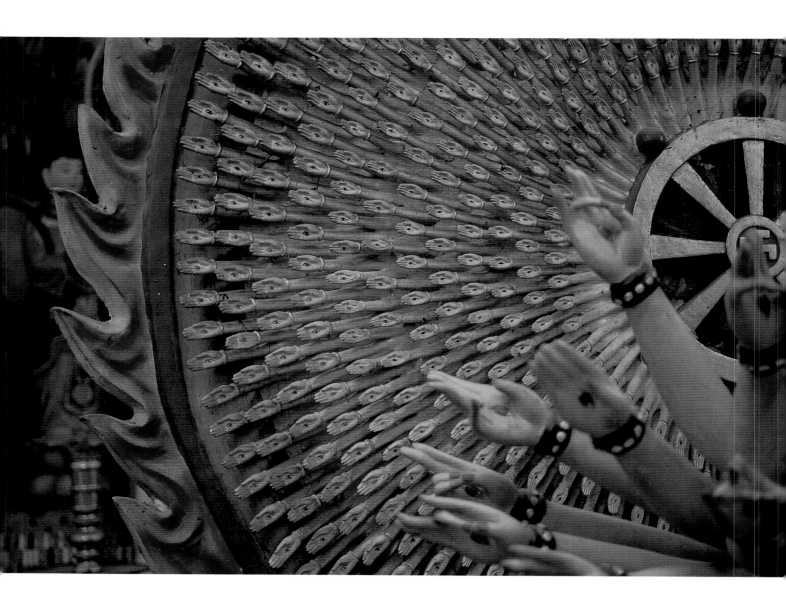

Wheel of law and helping hands. Part of a sculpture of
Avalokiteshvara in the Da Lam Co Tu pagoda (near Soc
Trang, Hau Giang Province)

RIGHT
Buddha and Bodhisattva. Statue of the many-armed
Avalokiteshvara on the altar of the Phat Hoc pagoda. Lying
underneath is the Sakyamuni on his way to Nirvana (Can
Tho, Hau Giang Province).

Water buffaloes in front of the Ba Ot *chua* on the Mekong Delta plains. The saddle roof and pointed ends of the roof ridges show the influence of neighbouring Cambodia. Right: Gateway to the memorial temple for the Mac princes who ruled the Cambodian border area and placed themselves under Vietnam's protection in the 18th century (near Ha Tien, Kien Giang Province).

193

Shoes and sandals slipped off on the steps to the Tam Bao pagoda. In the half-light of the altar room, a wishing tree decorated with simple Buddha figures and small lamps at which believers often pray for sick relatives to be healed (Ha Tien, Kien Giang Province).

RIGHT
Temple towers in the village of Xa Hoa Hung in the rice-growing area silhouetted against the rising sun (Cuu Long Province).

194

Donations for the upkeep of religious buildings. Red tissue paper receipt for the money donated by hundreds of thousands of Vietnamese believers.

Acknowledgments

Many people have helped us with this book: archaeologists and religious historians in Hanoi, Hue and Saigon, nuns, monks and novices all over Vietnam, archivists in France and America. But nothing can compare with the help we had from our drivers, Vinh, Le, Tang, Bac, Mao, Chin and Hien, who drove us thousands of miles safely, confidently and with unfailing good humour. No pre-dawn departure was too early for them, no path too narrow, no dyke too muddy, no ford too deep. Faced with situations that would have caused a pampered Westerner to despair - a broken axle in a remote mountain village, a carburettor damaged on a typhoon-flooded road - they never gave up. Without their determination and their local knowledge we would never have seen some of the secluded pagodas and community houses or tracked down hidden gems of Vietnamese religious art and the secrets and legends of their country's popular religion. We therefore owe them a special debt of gratitude.

The authors in Hanoi with their driver La Van Hien.

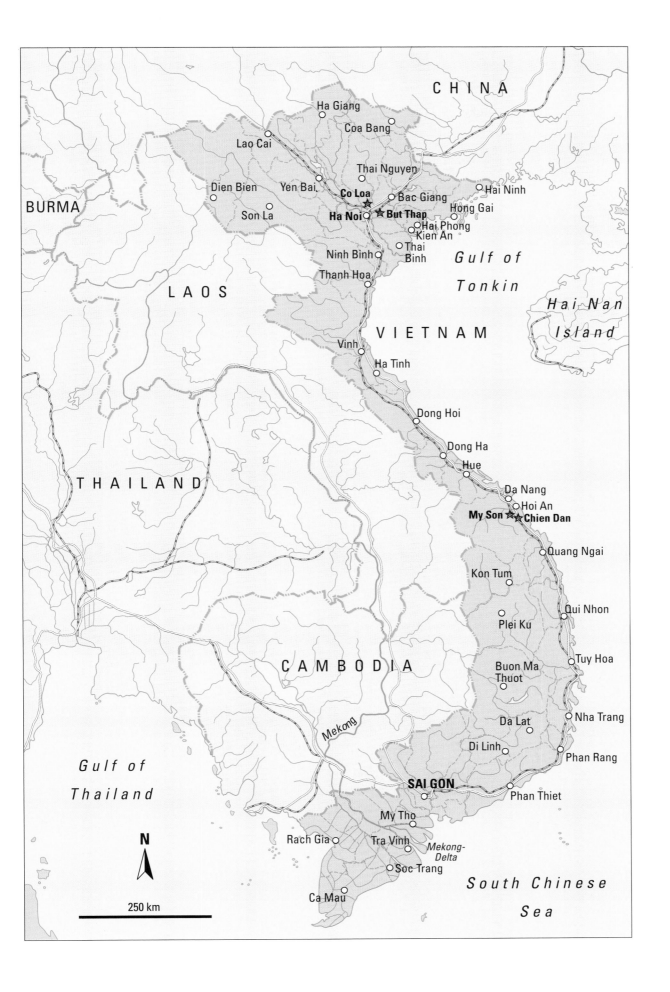

CHINA

Ha Giang

Coa Bang

Lao Cai

BURMA

Thai Nguyen

Dien Bien   Yen Bai
                   Co Loa   Hai Ninh
Son La   ☆   Bac Giang
                   Ha Noi ☆ **But Thap**   Hong Gai
                              Hai Phong
LAOS   Kien An
         Ninh Binh   Thai
                              Binh   *Gulf of*
         Thanh Hoa   *Tonkin*

                                                    Hai Nan
                   VIETNAM   *Island*

         Vinh
           Ha Tinh

THAILAND

                   Dong Hoi

                   Dong Ha
                     Hue
                       Da Nang
                       Hoi An
                   My Son ☆☆ **Chien Dan**

                              Quang Ngai

                   Kon Tum

CAMBODIA   Plei Ku   Qui Nhon

                                      Tuy Hoa
                   Buon Ma
                   Thuot
                              Nha Trang
                   Da Lat
         Mekong
                   Di Linh
                              Phan Rang
Gulf of   **SAI GON**
                              Phan Thiet
Thailand
                   My Tho

         Rach Gia Tra Vinh   *Mekong-*
                               Delta
N   Soc Trang
                                   South Chinese
         Ca Mau
250 km   *Sea*

Translated from the German *Vietnam: Gotter, Geister und Pagoden* by Lorna Dale

First Published in Great Britain in 1997
by Thames and Hudson Ltd, London

First published in the United States of America in hardcover
in 1997 by Thames and Hudson Inc., 500 Fifth Avenue,
New York, New York 10110

British Library Cataloguing-in-Publication Data

A catalogue record for this book is available from the
British Library

ISBN 0-500-01803-0

Library of Congress Catalog Card Number 97-60321

Printed and bound in Italy